OPEN MIC

A BROADCASTER'S MEMOIR

BIFF JANNUZZI

DEDICATION

To my parents, Matt and Leah Jannuzzi, who were there at the start of both me and my book. To Donna Polito, Bob Erck, Walt Marlowe, Ron Edwards and Art Hellyer who helped make this possible.

George E. Day: "You were tortured very hard and very heavily if you were caught communicating."

Barry Goldwater: "Now how do you think you got that period of grace? By Goldwater sitting on his can?"

Robert Conrad: "I'm 48 years old and movin'. I don't get the Travolta letters and I don't want 'em."

Red West: "This arm won't straighten out from falling on it so many times. This scar here was made by a piano that was supposed to break away and my head broke away instead. But it was fun. Pay was good. "

Kreskin: " I had to try to open the safe. There was only one problem. The only person who could think of the combination, who knew it, was the man who was inside the safe with 15 minutes air."

Jerald Agenbroad: "The three agents from the back of the truck opened up on the crowd and just in the general area with automatic weapon fire."

Jan Berry: "The recording is called 'Dead Man's Curve.' It was kind of an omen."

Ken Jacuzzi: "If you mention the name Jacuzzi, everybody automatically thinks you're extremely wealthy. It can really be a detriment to making an economical purchase at times."

Willie Tyler and Lester: "They'll accept it from him more so than they would me."

Joyce Brothers: "On "Family Feud" they asked, 'who are the ten greatest intellects, living or dead?' and I'm on the list...and that just surprised me."

Art Scholl: "They said, 'well he's the highest paid guy in Hollywood but he's the only one left alive'...and I thought...I've been doing this for quite a few years and I did look back and yes, all our other stunt pilots have been killed."

James "The Amazing" Randi: " A postman from San Francisco has now been healed of 11 different diseases by nine different faith healers in seven different cities in two genders...and...he has the healthiest ovaries of any postman in San Francisco."

Alabama: "If we took the fiddle out of the stuff we do, we'd probably have been on the pop charts in the '60s."

Cathy Rigby: "I don't know what the magic is exactly, except that they're so tiny and they do these incredible feats."

Meinhardt Raabe: "As coroner I must aver, I've thoroughly examined her and she's not only merely dead, she's really most sincerely dead."

Martha Reeves: "Vandella is a word derived after you're told if you don't get a name in 15 or 20 minutes you're gonna' be called anything."

Wolfman Jack: "They looked like nice folks and all of a sudden there's several people just wanting to make love to me."

Sonny Bono: "I wrote ten gold records and I produced a top three television show and now I'm standing here being bawled out by a midget."

Peter Noone: "Somebody thought I looked like Sherman, but we thought his name was Herman and I became Herman."

Steve Allen: "Somebody pointed out awhile back I'm the only comedian in show business who does not have an act."

James Lovell: "We were the first people to leave the Earth, essentially, and then see the far side of the Moon. The most thrilling flight, of course, was Apollo 13."

Fred Olivi: "You hear all kinds of stories. A lot of us are in the nut house and we're having all kinds of problems. Well, that's not true."

Robert Morgan: "I'd rather be up there than down here anytime."

Bill Winchell: "Right straight up, he hung it on its props...the props conk out, of course and then you're in a straight dive."

Lucas Brandolino: "Good thing the Lord held it up for 11 hours or we'd all have been down there someplace."

Bruno Rzonca: "All the body parts were laying on top of the deck...When the wave came by, the water was red of blood, so many guys."

Sebastian Junger: "He got a bad feeling, got off the boat and a month later he was watching the news...and it said the Andrea Gail was missing off... the Grand Banks and he said to his girlfriend, "'see? That was the boat I almost got on.'"

Erica Jong: "I think we're still teaching our children that sex equals death."

Karolyn Grimes: "Teacher says every time a bell rings, an angel gets his wings."

Johnnie Cochran Jr.: "There are a lot of things that I had, that I've handled that are more important to me, but at the same time, I suppose that (O.J.) Simpson and I will be forever intertwined."

Madeleine Brown: "Lyndon screamed in my ear that after tomorrow, being November the 22, the Kennedys...would never embarrass him again."

Tom Bodett: "It'll probably be chiseled on my tombstone and I've left in my will that if that happens I'm going to come back and haunt those people."

Margie McCauley: "Walking through there, it was like being in space."

Charles Hamilton: "I used to sell baseballs signed by Babe Ruth for $15 and today they bring $5000."

David Herbert Donald: "He raced up and down the White House stairs, three stairs at a time. He hallooed down the corridors. He enjoyed funny jokes with his secretaries. He liked his young wife who was ten years younger than he was and they had an active social life."

John Astin: "Gomez really, in a lot of ways, is just an extension of my own personality."

James Gregory: "I also, but keep this quiet, Biff, I slept in Marilyn Monroe's bed."

David Sanborn: "Everybody has their own definition of what jazz really is. I think people just need to lighten up."

THE BEST INTRODUCTION is the simple one. Book, reader, reader, book. Now that you know each other let me tell you what this book is about. It took many years to put together. You don't just sit down and write about people you've interviewed and known without that first critical step, that, of course, includes interviewing and knowing them. After that it's easier. As a reporter and writer working in media and hosting radio talk shows and interviewing hundreds of folks in a wide variety of life paths, a major benefit is meeting and talking with people you would never meet, if, for example, you were a grocery produce manager. Not that there's anything wrong with that job and there are some similarities. I've met some real vegetables working in radio. But these folks are not the vegetables. They are the cream at the top, the interesting folks; the ones who make the rest of us stand up and say, "are you somebody?"

Sometimes I've wondered if there is a common link among all of these people. Something we could point to and say, "okay, that's the key to career success." But I can't find that link. Many I talked to seemed very down to earth and often matter of fact about their accomplishments. As I look back, though, the only common ground that comes to mind is that none of them, from one of the first humans to see the Moon close up, to the man who played straight man to Cher, ever told me they were not good enough to have reached the success they did. I discovered gratitude for the success, but I never heard anyone say they didn't deserve it. That doesn't mean they didn't feel unworthy and maybe just wouldn't tell that to an interviewer. Certainly when being interviewed, they were, to one degree or another, in a "performance" mode and probably unlikely to speak negatively about their careers or achievements. Anyone on the reverse side (from my perspective) of the microphone would understandably have their guard up when being interviewed, even though, in most cases, I tried to keep it comfortable. So I can't say their apparent confidence is the key to big time fame or financial success or renown, but in the words of an old joke, "it couldn't hoit."

Along the way in this book, around the interviews, we'll take some side trips where I'll try to give you a feel for the blood, sweat and tears that went into this media career. No, I didn't interview that group. (Blood, Sweat and Tears, okay maybe I'm overexplaining) I don't know how many of them are even still around or performing and just blood and sweat aren't enough for a chapter, but I digress.

Keep in mind the context of the times for some of the interviews. Times and ideas change, so the views they express are snapshots of that moment. In the book, the more formal presentation of the interviews is intertwined with stories, thoughts, impressions, aggravations and sheer joy in the radio biz.

I hope you enjoy their stories at least as much as I enjoyed getting them to tell it, running it past the censors and attorneys, cutting out the objectionable and even slightly controversial, until I got this homogenized, sanitized version that will pass for truth. Actually, I left the good stuff in and only removed the references to Bob Dole and celery. Come to think of it, Bob Dole's mentioned too.

IT'S GLITZ, IT'S GLAMOUR, IT'S BROWN DIRT

I'D LIKE TO tell you a bit about my life and career. Not that either is over, at least as I write this. But you never know when that "check engine light" will come on and anything can end tomorrow, or this afternoon if it's ahead of schedule. So it's tenuous maybe, but not over. As we bounce around the radio trail I have to straighten something out. Maybe you think the radio biz is glamorous, with big salaries? Well, if you like bubbles and illusion, read no further. Oh, what the heck, go ahead and read. It's scary, but probably no worse than an evening with Bill Maher. I've never done that, but I have done radio. Please stay with us as we journey to the thrilling days of yesteryear. Radio is a roller coaster ride and like a roller coaster there are real highs and lows. Also, like a roller coaster ride, it's often gravity and momentum that keep you going. Whether a roller coaster or radio, the same advice applies. Don't stand directly under the kid with the green face.

There is an old joke about a man who was crazy. He thought he was a chicken. When they asked his wife why no one tried to get him some help, she replied, "well, we would, but we need the eggs." That pretty much explains why I stayed in radio. I know it's crazy, but I needed the eggs.

1977 was the momentous year. At age 25 I had my degree in Broadcasting from Arizona State University. That and a buck would buy a cup of coffee. Well, actually a presidential citation and a buck would also get you a cup as long as you left a tip. 1977 was also the year Elvis began his posthumous tour of Burger Kings and bowling alleys.

My first radio job was in Bisbee, Arizona. It's a small ex-mining (similar to ex-cavating but with bigger shovels) town, south of Tucson, Arizona, six miles from the Mexican border, then with about eight thousand friendly people who lived there for a variety of lifestyles. There were the hippies.

1977 was close enough to the 1960s you could still use that term. They lived in the "artists and others" part of town. There were the ex-miners, senior citizens, retirees and young families. A pretty good mix, unless you were single. In that case you hung around the convent hoping for dropouts.

March 31, KSUN and I was on the air for the first time. I actually wasn't on the payroll until April 1. That should have been a warning. I had been on radio, but never as an employee of a radio station. This time it was for real. My first night at the studio control board of KSUN was under the steady hand of Gene Butler. He was a station sales person, a great guy with a love of radio and who, unlike many of the people I would meet in radio over the years, had no out-of-control ego. I was lucky to start my career under Gene's guidance.

Now, I could tell you I sailed through the experience smoothly and effortlessly. I could also tell you I've spoken with Martians. Unfortunately,

I saved the damn tape that recorded my first time on KSUN in Bisbee and to my dismay, it reveals my shaky, high-pitched, nervous voice.

At a small station you have the blessing or maybe it's a curse of having a lot of different duties. I wrote ad copy, helped with the news and played disc jockey with a country western format. Biff and country western -- an oxymoron -- like rap music. After all, I grew up liking Burt Bacharach and the Carpenters and the Fifth Dimension. Three months after I began the job, the news director quit and went home to Missouri. I got his job, the office and the fun assignments, including the time the Mexican sewage treatment plant six miles away, just across the Mexican border, filled to capacity with rainwater. That resulted in sewage overflowing across the border into the flat, and now brown-stained desert floor on the U.S. side. A city official and I walked the area and went under the fence to get closer to the plant. How often have you heard of people going under the fence into Mexico? As I recall, unlike some sections of the border, this fence wasn't more than some wire.

So here we are in Bisbee, Arizona in 1977 and '78. At least I am, or was. I'm working my first radio job and have been promoted to news director. That meant my salary jumped $50 a month to a whopping $400 a month. This is not a joke. I know because I will tell a few in this book and you'll be able to compare. Rent was only $120 a month so I could live on $400, but it was a sign of salaries to come. That too should have been a warning!

My apartment building had its own history as an old schoolhouse they stopped using as a school in the 1930s. The White House Club and Apartments later became a Bed and Breakfast. That was after I left Bisbee. In 1977-78, two of us from the radio station lived there in the back apartments. We were also told this three-story building between two bluffs was a landmark for the drug smuggling planes coming up from Mexico. They would see our building and know they were over the "line" and back in the U.S.

ROCK STARS AND DEAD PEOPLE

AS WITH ANY topflight news reporter I was right on top of the story the day in August 1977 when Elvis allegedly died. I say allegedly, of course, because he was sighted at the Bisbee Sonic Drive-In two weeks after that and months before he began his posthumous tour. That is a joke. Or is it?

Anyway, the day his death was announced I knew it right away. Is that because I was news director and had my finger on America's pulse? No, it's because Program Director Lee Akers came around the corner into my office and said, "Presley's dead." I certainly didn't learn that from the wire service. Our station owner, disputing his bill with United Press International, had his service cut off -- a painful act at best -- and so the wire machine was just tapping away without printing a word. No doubt we were one of the few newsrooms in the world with a wire machine and no notice of the "King" shuffling off. Long live bill collectors. The news service had left the building.

As I made my morning news runs to gather stories I used to stop every day for coffee. I'd go to the county offices and to the police station to see what was going on and I'd stop in at my friend Harry's body shop, as in mortuary. Years later I still remember his coffee was quite strong. But then again, in a funeral home you don't want to be caught drowsing. You nod off and suddenly your family gets a bill.

We would visit upstairs above the "parlor" and a few feet from the "workroom." One day I stopped in and there was Harry's friend, Richard Wright from the rock group Pink Floyd. Very alive. I had seen him earlier in his visit to a local bar. This time at Harry's, he was clearly freaked out, as we used to say, about being in a funeral home.

He talked about his home in Colorado and I think Europe too and since he wanted to go to a bar in the Brewery Gulch section of old Bisbee, I dropped him off. Never saw him again. He didn't disappear in Bisbee; he just never wrote or called. Imagine that! We had shared such a bond. I had always been taught that if you want to fuse a friendship, share coffee in a funeral parlor. I continued making my $400 a month on the dark side of the moon and presumably he went home to Aspen.

Even years before my first radio job, the "interview bug," if there is such a thing, had bitten me. In 1974 I interviewed a returned Vietnam prisoner of war. Today if you see a Vietnam Vet being interviewed you can expect to see an older person. But 1974 was not that far removed from Vietnam and we Baby Boomers still had dark hair and we as a nation had not come to terms with the war.

GEORGE E. "BUD" DAY

"Your windows were boarded up and your day was one of absolute boredom and total introspection...You were tortured very hard and very heavily if you were caught communicating."

George E. "Bud" Day was happy to arrive in Vietnam. It was 1967 and the Air Force pilot felt he should be there. He had many years of fighter pilot experience and felt an obligation to his country to take part in what was both a ground and fighter war. Most of his fellow fighter pilots were going to Vietnam. What he might have suspected but couldn't know was just how much sacrifice that obligation would require of him and how long it would be before he returned home.

When I interviewed him in 1974, Day told me he arrived in Vietnam around April 1, 1967. It was a rather non-specific answer. When I asked him when his jet was shot down, though, Day was right to the point. "I was shot down August 26 of '67." Day's plane was striking a missile site near the Demilitarized Zone or DMZ that separated North and South Vietnam. He said, "I was in an operation which was designed to locate targets of opportunity." His procedure was to "search out these targets and then bring in fighters, put them in on the target, observe the bombing accuracy, photograph it if possible." Day made a pass across the missile site, didn't find it, and said, "because you don't make two passes in a row across a target of that nature I went on up and put some strikes in another area." Day flew out to the tanker and when he made a pass across the target a second time he got hit, "quite hard in the controls of the airplane. It went out of control and I was forced to eject."

A day that began normally had just taken a spiral into a hell relatively few Americans will experience and one that would last for years. He was floating by parachute to earth unconscious above North Vietnam and it would be nearly five and a half years before he would leave that country. His capture came within about 60 to 90 seconds after he gained consciousness on the ground. "I had been broken up in the bailout, somewhat. My right arm was pretty badly injured," and he had other wounds.

The names of the prisoner of war camps in North Vietnam reflected a certain spirit of the POWs and Day spent time in many of them. They included Heartbreak Hotel, Little Vegas, which was also called the Hilton, as well as Plantation, the Zoo and camps called Skid Row and Camp Unity. There was a large number of the prisoners of war divided among the camps and Day said "the idea behind that was to keep us split up into small groups, keep us divided, keep us exploitable. It's a lot easier to exploit a small group than it is a large one." Day pointed out "there's strength in numbers."

Propaganda was a regular part of the POWs' days. "Our news was all managed." The only source was communist radio. There was a small speaker in every room. "You were played a half hour of propaganda broadcast in the morning, again at night and then once during the day you got an hour of indoctrination." World War Two Allied troops had to put up with the propaganda programs of Axis Sally. Vietnam had what the prisoners called Hanoi Hanna, what they called fairy tales or science fiction hour. Day said it was "very, very distorted and incredible recitations of what was going on in the world, in the communist world and in America. Very unfactual, very crude, very unbelievable." Everything you got was politically slanted to make you feel bad, to cause anxiety, adding, "it was communist brainwashing." Day was not given anything to read generally throughout the years he was a POW until about 1972, but there was never any open source of news other than propaganda literature that pictured the U.S. as the villain in Southeast Asia. If you weren't hearing a Vietnamese on the radio, all you heard "were anti-war types of the Sloan Coffin, Ramsey Clark, Jane Fonda, this ilk -- everyone who, of course, was crusading anti-American."

There was no work in the prison camps to keep them busy. If you were in solitary, you sat and looked at four walls. "Your windows were boarded up. Your door was boarded up. Your day was one of absolute boredom and total introspection. That was your only source of amusement. There was no outside time, no exercise time, very little contact with anyone... very, very difficult psychological conditions." Communication was forbidden. "You were tortured very hard and very heavily if you were caught communicating." You could talk to a roommate if you got along with them, but Day said, "one of the problems involved with this was if you had a bad roommate," that he pointed out, "could also be kind of a special hell. There were some people who did not bear up well." He noted there were some "marvelous relationships" but there were also some that were very unpleasant.

If you were around during the Vietnam era, or have studied the history, you probably remember the controversy over actress Jane Fonda's visit to North Vietnam. It earned her the nickname Hanoi Jane and the contempt of Colonel Day.

Day told me, "the first thing you have to understand about any visitor to one of those culturally deprived countries is that they have to be pro that country or they don't get in." Day said it's natural they would come out of North Vietnam and report what they already believed going in. "We were personally very disappointed and very discouraged with the fact that Americans were actively working against America. We felt it was disloyal. We felt it was treasonous."

In November of 1970, the U.S. conducted a raid on a POW camp. It was, as Day recalled, a "very high day for POWs." There was no one in the camp when the rescue team arrived, but despite that, Day said it was "beautifully executed." He added, "it forced and terrorized the Vietnamese into moving us from all of these small and diverse outlying camps into a central camp. They had no choice but to put us into one central prison and as a result many people who had been solo for more than four years now had roommates and it brought a tremendous change of treatment." You can't treat a group of around 40 people in the same harsh ways you can treat one person because, Day said, "40 people won't put up with it, whereas one person may have to."

The POWs' environment went from a "limbo" where they had no chance to study or use their time to where they now could organize classes and church. "We immediately began using our days in a totally useful way all day." Before that, for the POWs, the 16 or 18 hours days were a waste.

When the U.S. mined Haiphong Harbor in 1972, Day and others at his camp saw the food quality drop substantially. "It immediately cut off the outside food supply which the Vietnamese relied on very heavily, both for themselves and for us. However, we welcomed it because we could see that the end was in sight. This was one of the natural steps that had to have been taken in order to bring (the war) to a halt."

Operation Linebacker occurred in late December 1972, a large scale bombing by the U.S. Air Force. Day and others could tell from the bombing patterns that B-52s were involved. About 15 minutes after it began, "we knew we were free men then." The POWs didn't know when they would be released, "but we knew when the bombing stopped that the Vietnamese would capitulate." Day had been a squadron commander at the prison camp known as Camp Unity, but he had been relieved of that command by the North Vietnamese because they didn't like the fact the POWs under his command were cheering about the bombing. The "V" as Day called them, objected to the POWs' excitement over the killing of Vietnamese. They put him in a small group that was living under hard conditions.

The POWs heard about the signing of the so-called protocols on January 28, 1973 and the next day they got a copy that detailed the release order. When he was finally released from captivity, Day returned to March Field in California and from there entered a society that was a far cry from life in North Vietnamese prisons. "I was immediately impressed again with what a high speed society we are." He added, "technology moves along so rapidly and it's a very quick moving world, and when you haven't been a part of it for a long time, why it seems as if it's just almost going at an overwhelming pace. But interestingly enough you get used to that very quickly." Returning home in 1973, Day was disturbed by what he saw as changes for the worse in the country, including the amount of drug abuse.

Day's meeting with President Nixon was a highlight of his return and an emotional experience. He said, "(Nixon) was the man upon whom the decision to bomb Hanoi ultimately rested and as Harry Truman said, 'the buck stops here.'" Day said, "despite all of the criticism which was leveled against (Nixon) for bombing Hanoi, that was absolutely the only way he was going to get the prisoners out. He knew it, we knew it, the Vietnamese knew it."

Having served in three wars, Day was in a special position to compare the different experiences of the returning veteran. In World War Two he was "30 months in the Pacific...and when I came back it was a feeling of great satisfaction in the country. We'd gone from a semi-industrialized, semi-developed status into a fantastically highly developed economy, highly developed industrial capacity." Day said he was being blunt by stating "for practical purposes we bailed England and France out totally... and according to me, carried the war." He said veterans were received with "great welcome and with great respect and so it was a very, very fine homecoming. Everyone felt a tremendous sense of satisfaction."

In the 1950s, Day was off to the Far East for his duty in the Korean War. Day told me the objective of that war was not clear to the troops and he suspected not very clear to the nation's leaders at times. It also lasted too long, according to Day, which he saw as the war's greatest fault. He said some saw it as a kind of World War Two and some returning vets were received very well, but others felt the war was a waste for the country. In general though, Day felt most Korean War vets were received quite well. Vietnam was a different story. In our 1974 interview Day noted there wasn't anywhere near the concern or the compassion or interest by the general public in the Vietnam vet, "perhaps because there's so many of them and it lasted so long. I think that perhaps that might be a hazard of a modern nation attempting 20 year wars." Day wasn't a POW in World War Two or Korea, and he didn't get the letters from strange people he got after his POW experience in Vietnam. When we talked, nearly all of the letters he had received expressed happiness he was back and wished him well. But he also had four or five of what he called unsigned, nutsy letters. That, said Day, "probably would not have happened in World War Two" but he admitted, "I may be wrong."

After his return from Vietnam, Day became actively involved with the POW organization and the Missing In Action group trying to get an accounting from North Vietnam on what happened to the MIAs. He went on to publish his own book, "Return With Honor." For several months shortly after his return to the U.S. he was on the go from five in the morning to 11 at night every day, seven days a week. "But of course, after looking at four walls for many years, it was a great pleasure, and there was no greater place in the world to do it in than here."

Day had an interesting story to tell and I should have kept that in mind years later when I landed in my first radio job in Bisbee. It would have been a good lesson for the time I found myself at a loss for words.

THE REPORTER SPEAKS.
THE REPORTER HAS NOTHING TO SAY

DURING THAT FIRST radio job in Bisbee I decided to be a guest speaker. It was one of my first attempts at local celebrity. I was invited to talk to inmates at the Cochise County jail. My main memory is one inmate asking me to describe my most memorable experience in radio. That was my first lesson in celebrity status. You have to have something interesting to say. I had been in radio only a short time. My most memorable experience so far was the drive down from Phoenix. So I took record requests from the "audience." So much for stardom.

Bisbee celebrated Claims Day; a celebration of the town's first mining claim, and that got me a certain amount of community recognition. That year it was the 100th anniversary. Those of us from the radio station walked in a parade in the old section of town, through the canyon of hills, houses and businesses. We had 45-rpm records to toss to the parade watchers. If you're really young I should explain that's not the number of records we had. That was a type of record. It played at 45 rpm. That's revolutions per minute and the records were black vinyl, most of them and...oh just go ask your parents or grandparents or take a trip to the museum.

Centennial parade

Bisbee Fire Chief Clyde Burchinal gives Mayor Chuck Eads a tour of Main Street in the city's 1915 American LaFrance fire engine during the Claim's Day Centennial parade Saturday. The parade and other festivities celebrated the 100th anniversary of the first mining claim, a silver strike, filed in the Bisbee area. The fire truck is one of Bisbee's original mechanized fire engines. For other photos of the weekend celebration, see pages 2 and 3. (Staff photo by Orazio Fresina.)

**It's hard to see but I'm actually in this photo,
walking behind the flag bearers**

Anyway, I remember tossing the records up to people in the second story above the parade route. Thinking back, that probably was dangerous. I never heard of any decapitations, though, and if there had been, I'm sure heads would have rolled.

After a year in Bisbee I had accumulated some memorable moments. One was traveling the area with the Harlem Globetrotters. Curly Neal, Meadowlark Lemon and Marques Haynes were still part of the group and they trained at the Fort Huachuca Army base in the nearby town of Sierra Vista.

Meadowlark told me he could perform ten minutes of routine based just on someone in the audience dropping a bottle of pop (fyi, that's also soda.) While at the Fort fieldhouse they performed a couple of basketball games over two days for television taping. Do you think the Globetrotters were ever the same after Curly and Meadowlark left?

If someone didn't like me, they should have just told me. Instead, one day Program Director Akers tells me a call had come in and someone had said there was a bomb for Biff Jannuzzi and the KSUN staff. The husband and wife who ran the station had gone to lunch. I'm glad at least the program director told me. As you can tell, I did not end up blown and scattered to the winds. We figured the bomb caller was joking. I didn't think it was funny.

To take part in the local flavor, we spent one day broadcasting live from the grand opening of the Queen Mine Tour. The tour is an underground excursion into the side of the mountain where there once had been a working copper mine. For me it was an all-day session of interviews and filling time with music from the event while I corralled interviewees.

It all prepared me to think on my feet and made me a better interviewer. I don't have any tape of the day but I probably would wince at how banal some of the interviews must have been. I do have a picture of me interviewing the head of the chamber of commerce. He once told me that his professed love for the area was a front. He was not overly thrilled with Bisbee. Maybe that made me an even more skeptical interviewer. That's a valuable lesson in radio and a lot of the business world, a world in which radio definitely belongs, specifically that not everything is what it seems. Much of the glamour is outside the radio station door. You'd understand that even more if you toured some of your local radio stations in a smaller market. A trailer by the side of the road and a couple of grungy rooms may be all you would find. Just a control board and an antenna in some cases or a "board and a stick" as one radio veteran described it.

You may be able to tell who's in the radio station at any given time by the type of car in the parking lot. If the beater is there, then the afternoon DJ is on duty. The luxury car with the leather seats means the manager and/ or owner is in. The relatively nice functional car is a sign the sales guy is there. Reading parking lots is an art form that I'm afraid will be lost.

NO SCREAMING AS YOU LEAVE THE PLANE. BUH-BYE

EVER JUMP FROM a perfectly good airplane? It's amazing what a single bored person and, of course, a single, bored person does for fun, even if you do get a radio feature story out of it. Think of jumping off the roof of a house. It has nothing to do with skydiving but it's a fun image, huh? Actually, it does have a connection. So now think of being surrounded in soft silk, floating to earth. Okay, now think of driving 40 miles an hour past a toxic waste dump with three screaming kids and... well, for now we'll stick to skydiving. My, how your mind does wander.

I wanted to try something different. How would you define "different?" To me, skydiving is a good answer. A silly answer, maybe. I joined a small group out of the nearby town of Sierra Vista for one day of training, jumping and X-rays. No, wait, the X-rays came the next day, so I guess it was a two-day activity. After several hours of learning how to land and roll we were ready to go, or so I thought. The training had not prepared me for the jolt of the contact with the ground.

We were told how to get out of the main chute if, by chance, we looked up and saw a hole in the main, and had to open the reserve chute. In our training, we also learned about one skydiver who, once the main chute was in trouble, tried to go for the reserve and couldn't get it open, clawing with his hands all the way down. And I mean all the way down. When they found the body; (pausing here for effect), well, I don't want to get too graphic. Actually I do, but you could be eating and considering the cost of lunch and maybe drycleaning...Write me and I'll send the details.

There were three of us "daredevils" in our planeload o' jumpers. The small plane was a four-seater with three of the seats taken out. They kindly left one for our pilot. Under ideal conditions the pilot would not be jumping this day. So the three of us, including a jumpmaster, also riding on the floor, and the pilot (on the port side), took off for three thousand feet. It was a podiatrist convention. (Insert rimshot here.) See, feet? Podiatrist? Well it just isn't the same if I have to explain.

I don't remember being too nervous. It seems ignorance really is bliss. In this small plane they also remove the starboard door, on the right side, opposite the pilot. I didn't want to sit next to that opening! I mean, I might fall out! Don't they think of that? I'm not sure if I have a fear of heights or it's a fear of falling, but at this point I wasn't trying to decide. Of course if I did fall out, I'd have a parachute. That's some consolation. In this case, though, my "adventure" was what's called a static line jump. The ripcord is attached to the floor of the plane, much like my fingernails, and is automatically pulled when you leave the plane, much like my fingernails. That's not the only automatic reaction when you leave a perfectly good airplane but that's for the medical books. So the first guy went out the starboard side...a big guy, somewhat portly. Seemed to me it would be safer for me to land on him.

Then it was my turn. I moved up on the floor of the plane. I was to the right of the pilot, (or starboard side as we in-the-know types know, no?) next to the gaping hole where the door had been. During the flight I had stayed back from it. Now I turned to my right and dangled my legs in the wind and grabbed the strut of the overhead wing, pulling myself up with the help of an attached step. You also can use the wheel of the plane next to the step. They make it so damn convenient, don't you think? When you pull yourself out and stand facing forward into the wind, among your thoughts is, "I'm standing outside an airplane!" This is not natural. If you think so, consider how many times you say it in everyday conversation. As long as you're thinking odd things, think of the great people in history who made a mark without ever experiencing that. Lincoln never got an aerial view of the Capitol. He never opened a car door and he never typed a letter. He never saw a "No Right Turn" sign. Either did I that one time and the cop said...well, okay, that's another story. Abe couldn't tell you what a dishwasher was. He didn't understand indoor plumbing. I think I've made my point, and then some.

What can prepare you for hanging onto a plane strut? Maybe sitting on the hood of a car, at 75 miles an hour? However, a parachute wouldn't help in the five feet between the car and the street, unless, of course, you're driving at three thousand feet. I could have turned around and gone back inside the plane, but what the heck. The guy on the ski jump in that old film at the opening of "Wide World of Sports" probably had doubts too, or maybe he figured as long as he was up there he may as well go down. Where did it get him? He was humiliated every Saturday afternoon by the film of his fall down the ski jump as the show's opening video pitched the "thrill of victory" but yes, also the "agony of defeat."

Do you like the way I casually use the words starboard and port talking about the plane? Here's a way to impress your friends and bore enemies. Personally I've never borne enemies, but it can't be as hard as bearing children and I can't bear children either. I wish I could, but then, I wish I could stop this free association too, because, nothing is free, unless it's lunch and even then there's a tip. What was the question? Oh, yes, here's a way to tell port from starboard. Port is left and starboard is right. No, that's not specific enough. Okay, port and left both have four letters. Ta dah!

Our jumpmaster said "go." Not wanting to rush this, I cleverly stalled and said "what?" He wouldn't be dissuaded. He repeated, "go!" So I departed a perfectly good airplane. You're supposed to simulate pulling the ripcord, to get used to the idea, although the actual ripcord is attached to the plane and automatically pulled for you as you leave the plane and the chute opens almost immediately. If you've jumped, you know that the term "static line jump" does not refer to the argument you give the jumpmaster before leaving. There was no freefall in this, no falling thousands of feet unencumbered. That comes after you've mastered the static line jump. However, that first jump was my one and only attempt.

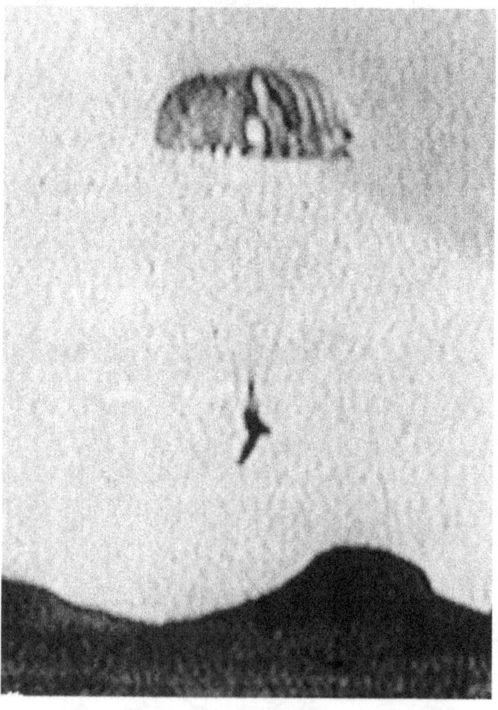

I must have been nervous because I remember breathing heavily. I looked up at the chute. It was a round and a now obsolete style, because today they're rectangular and winged shape and much more "flyable." We were told to pull the reserve parachute if something went wrong with the main. Of course, before jumping, we were advised that foreign matter, which in Arizona could be something like mesquite wood, could rip a hole in the main chute. All these wonderful tales gave me so much confidence.

My photos are from a video transfer of Super 8 movie film showing my departure from the plane and part of the descent to the desert floor. One look at the profile of me in the film and it's no surprise the landing was such a jolt. I was nearly z-shaped. You could almost slip a chair under me. Come to think of it, a large Lazy Boy would have really softened the fall. I know now my scrunching up before landing, while maybe a natural reaction, creates an unnatural landing. As I descended, I had all I could do to keep from drifting away from the small airport. Mexico is only a few miles south. How do I explain just dropping in? Buenos dias, uh, yo Americano drifter. Si, from the sky. One of the three in our jump group landed in a tree and I think he broke a small bone in his foot. I landed with the ease of a Chevy. I could have said Chrysler but my brother Alan spent his career with General Motors and there would have gone the sale of one copy of this book.

The landing knocked the wind right out of me. In training, they told us how to get out of the main chute, if necessary, while we descended. Even after I landed I still couldn't release it. So there I was on the ground, gasping for air, surrounded by silk. Sounds erotic doesn't it? It wasn't. The ground crew came out to pick me up. The next day I was still having trouble with my back muscles, which had decided to teach me a lesson about banging them around like that. I went to the local emergency room for X-rays. (You thought I was kidding about that.) No damage done, other than the cost of the X-rays. Fortunately my insurance paid the $112.00. Today that would probably be pretty cheap.

I expected my landing to be the equivalent of jumping off a window ledge. Wrong! Instead, maybe because of my Z-shaped descent, it was more like jumping off the roof of a house. The moral is, if you jump from a plane and land wrong and scrunch up your back and gasp for air and pay good money for it, you'll have a nifty story to tell on the air the next day and also years later. (See?)

WHEN WILLIAM SHATNER WAS HERE, SPIDERS RULED THE VALLEY. IT WAS ONLY A MOVIE, RIGHT?

VERDE (PRONOUNCED VAIR-DAY, or as the anglicized version would sound, VUR-dee) means green, as in "escaping suburbanites' money." The small town of Cottonwood, Arizona, north of Phoenix in the Verde Valley, has continued to grow into more of a haven for escaping Phoenicians. William Shatner was here a few years before to film "Kingdom of the Spiders," where spiders took over the Valley. If they did, all traces of that menace were gone when I got there. I lived in the Cottonwood "suburb" of Clarkdale, an even smaller town. My apartment was above an old theater in an old brick building next to a park with a gazebo. In the early morning (and I would see far too many early mornings in the radio years to come) I could look out my west window and see the lights of a town you may have heard of called Jerome, perched high on the side of Mingus Mountain. Jerome used to promote itself as a ghost town. That caricature worked for the tourists even though the residents were less than "ghostlike."

My job, for a month, was at KVRD; VRD, as in Verde. Stations just love tie-ins like that to the local area. The work included signing the station on the air at six a.m., which just meant turning on the transmitter and taking meter readings, making news rounds in the morning and filling in on the morning talk show, where I would rely on odd stories from the news wirecopy. This was actually my first talk show. Thank goodness I got better at it. Then I would spend the afternoon until five p.m. selling airtime to advertisers. Looking back on my early radio days, I don't think I paid much attention to the number of daily hours I put in during my first radio job in Bisbee. Now three years later in Cottonwood, I began to notice. The lesson has pretty much been learned now. Can you understand why it's hard to keep good people in radio?

KVRD in Cottonwood in the Verde Valley was my first experience with full station automation with recorded music tape reels and programmed commercials. This particular automation unit would also tell time for the listeners. At the time (no pun intended) I thought that was very fancy, except the station manager told me for the cost of that unit it would have been cheaper to buy everyone in Cottonwood a watch. In 1980, automation, with its recorded music and weather and computer-timed playing of commercials, was the beginning of the end for a lot of radio jobs, what I would say was the first serious step in that direction. Even worse threats to the jobs were coming. These were pre-satellite days. In later years, satellite services such as Satellite Music Network put one DJ in a network studio and he or she pretended to be in your town. For local flavor the station could play recordings of the DJ saying local "liners" such as "your best music for a Saturday night, KXXX, right here in the heart of artichoke country." It's an unstoppable trend of fewer people, more buttons and less local personality radio. Local news, however, is tough to provide by satellite, so news is a little more automation and satellite-proof than the music and clever DJ patter.

If your favorite station was satellite programming, you could listen for little clues, such as the time checks or announcements. You wouldn't hear the hour. It would be 22 minutes past the hour, or 15 minutes before the top of the hour, since the broacast is crossing time zones. You also might have noticed a current temperature in the weather forecast, but in a different voice. If you really had a discerning ear, you might have caught a tonal quality difference between the live voice and the local recorded tie-ins.

Since I was once again being forced to do sales at a station, and just thrilled to do that (insert sarcasm here), it's not surprising I left KVRD after a month. Actually I received a call from KVOY AM/ KJOK FM in Yuma in the southwestern corrner of Arizona, on my first day on the job at KVRD, asking if I were interested in working in Yuma. I was and so I followed up on that lead and I was off to Yuma.

KVOY AM and KJOK FM in Yuma were established stations. You know what I mean; the traditional or standard stations people think of when they think of an area. I spent one year at that AM/FM combo and learned a lot. That's very good because I knew very little when I got to Yuma, so I could only improve, even after my book-larnin' degree from Arizona State University and experience at the small stations in Bisbee and Cottonwood.

The "news closet" for delivering newscasts at KVOY Yuma. And you thought it was glamorous behind the scenes

When I started at KVOY/KJOK in Yuma they wanted me to use my real first name. I've never been fond of using the name Judy on the air. Just kidding, actually it's Phyllis. No really it's Bernard, but that's too formal. Incidentally, I pronounce it BERnard, not BerNARD. I thank you. That reminds me of the joke where the star is Johnny Sparkle. Someone says that can't be his real name and he agrees, saying it's Sidney Sparkle. Well, Jannuzzi is my real name and "Biff" is my real lifelong nickname, but since "Biff" didn't give them the sound they wanted, they said it had to be Bernard, which is silly 'cause my real name is Eileen. That's another joke. I know it is because I've heard jokes and that sounded just like one. Hmmm, Eileen Jannuzzi. Nope, not the right on-air image. Not bad for some parties but that's another story and thankfully one that I'm not qualified to tell anyway.

This was the AM radio station KJOK in all its automated glory

One of my tasks was to go into the streets and beg for money for the station. Okay, again not really. See? You let one joke in and others just invade your space; totally, dude. Actually, I was on the street to get interviews of public opinion. We called it Voices of Yuma. To say I hated it would be...actually correct. I usually headed for the shopping mall to collect my ten-second sound bites from people on general news topics. I asked one man if I could interrupt his reading. He kept his head down and shook his head. Some would talk, but others shied away from the mike. Another man was unintelligible, twice. Another woman stopped me before I even got the question out. She wasn't sure she should talk to me. She said she'd been drinking. Somehow, though, I always got enough sober comments to make up the feature.

My experience with Mexican/U.S. border towns along the Arizona and California borders has not always been favorable, but the towns are fascinating. The Mexican cities were often larger than their American counterparts just north, across the line. In the early 1980s, San Luis, Sonora, Mexico had about 120,000 people and in the 2015 Census it was closing in on 200,000. In contrast, San Luis, Arizona, on the north side of the border, was a smaller town, though by 2014 its population topped 31,000. If you were looking for leather, liquor or velvet paintings, San Luis, Sonora, Mexico was the place to be. You could haggle with the merchants, but you quickly realized they knew their bottom line. Still, it was silly to accept the first price, silly and needlessly expensive.

Miguel de la Madrid was about to become the new president of Mexico when he visited San Luis, Sonora in 1981. Without the language skills of our Spanish Program Director Frank Preciado I would have been at a total loss.

In my four years in Yuma I drove my car into Mexico only once. That was for an international game of softball between radio station employees from San Luis, Sonora and Yuma. Most times I visited I parked on the U.S. side and walked across. I was nervous, like many Americans I suppose. There were stories of arrests from the Mexican federales for something as simple as a traffic accident and tales of people who are never seen again. On the other hand, you regularly hear stories of people disappearing in the United States, too.

Okay, so I spent time in a Mexican penitentiary. What's it to ya'? (Did that get your attention?) By this time I had moved from KVOY/KJOK across town to the NPR member station KAWC at Arizona Western College as the News Producer, working with students and covering stories. Actually a fellow reporter from my old station and I wanted to tour the prison in San Luis, Mexico. We made arrangements and drove in his car to the facility, following behind the coordinator of our visit. Naturally we got a little nervous on the way when he pulled to the side of the road and stopped. We pulled over behind him. Were we about to be abducted and tossed into the prison, never to be seen again? (Those horror stories again!) Relax. Our guide had just stopped to talk with someone he knew. Does it pay to be paranoid? Probably not even minimum wage. Arriving at the prison we met briefly with the warden and began our tour. The prison or Re-Adaptation Center as they preferred to call it, was remarkably clean, perhaps in anticipation of our visit. We witnessed a training class, and some beautiful wood products made there and we talked with a couple of American prisoners. One American was there for smuggling over 400 pounds of marijuana while another said he transported guns across the border to trade for gasoline. The gun owner felt the prison time was "easy time" and not as crowded as American jails. The drug smuggler was bored, but felt his prison conditions were better than anything he had heard about Mexican jails. I doubt the two men are still there. It's been decades. I hope they're not, but stranger things have happened.

**Guarding the gates at the Mexican penitentiary,
San Luis, Sonora, Mexico.**

While it's not always true, the bigger market gives a better chance to meet and greet and interview celebrities. Yuma wasn't a big city but compared to Cottonwood it was a bustling metropolis. Anyway it was big enough to have visits from the state's top politicians and that included Arizona's own (and nationally known) Republican Senator Barry Goldwater.

BARRY GOLDWATER

"I might say I just got word that your post office is going to stay where it is for three more years. Now how do you think you got that period of grace? By Goldwater sitting on his can...?"

I think it's true that all politics is local. Arizona Senator and 1964 Republican presidential candidate Barry Goldwater could keep it local, as he did when he told reporters in Yuma about a reprieve for a local post office. But Barry Goldwater had a way about him, a directness that worked for him. This particular press conference came as he ran for reelection to the Senate in 1980. He dismissed his opponent's complaint that Goldwater wasn't present when votes were taken in the Senate. Goldwater pointed out it was more important to be on the job than on the Senate floor. He stated,"where would you rather have me? Spending a whole day on the Senate floor making maybe five, ten, or even 18 votes on nothing, or have me downtown talking to the Post Office as I've been doing, and I might say I just got word that your post office is going to stay where it is for three more years. Now how do you think you got that period of grace? By Goldwater sitting on his can on the Senate floor or Goldwater down at the Post Office department saying 'look, here's the problem in Yuma?'"

Goldwater could be funny while making a point. He said Arizona voters wanted someone who had on-the-job ability. For example, if there were a controversy with the military and Mexico, "I'm much better off going down to see the ambassador of Mexico and saying, 'look my good friend, I know a few rockets landed in Northern Mexico yesterday but the wind was a little strong.'"

In 1980 it had been 16 years since Goldwater carried the Republican Party into the presidential battle against Democrat and then-incumbent President Lyndon Johnson. Johnson won by a landslide. Now, besides his own Senate race in 1980, Goldwater was campaigning for presidential candidate and fellow Republican Ronald Reagan, but Goldwater was limiting that work to Arizona.

I asked the senator how presidential campaigning had changed. Remember this was back in 1980 when he said, "well, there's a lot more of what we call Madison Avenue. The appearances are far more expertly staged." He added, "while I ran against a man whose honesty I wouldn't have vouched for (Johnson), Reagan's running against the most dishonest man I've ever known in my political life, and I've been around the politics of this country for many and many a year. (Jimmy) Carter just doesn't have it in him to be honest."

Goldwater said a major reason why he was campaigning for Ronald Reagan in the 1980 presidential race (which Reagan won) was Reagan's promise to "diminish the controls of the federal government over the business of this country." Goldwater added, "if he does nothing else it will mean more business and better business, more profits, more people working than the way we're going today."

Goldwater blamed then-President Carter for not having a foreign strategy. "Had we had a foreign policy and had we had the military strength, I don't think we would have ever seen Iran take one single American boy as a hostage." He said, "we've got to have a foreign policy and Carter doesn't have either the brains or, pardon me, the guts to create a foreign policy." Once again, Goldwater was clear about his views. You might not have liked his opinions but he could be direct.

Goldwater's long political career must have taken him to countless dinners and speeches and along what has been called the "rubber chicken" circuit. I asked him about that when we met again in Yuma as he campaigned for a local candidate. He said he had a map on the wall with pins where he had traveled. It had fallen down. At that same political gathering my microphone was taped to the mike stand on a lectern but I hadn't secured it well. As you can see in the photo, it drooped, until eventually it fell during his speech.

Barry Goldwater and my drooping microphone

Goldwater said, in effect, that it was okay, that worse things had happened, and he took the mike and put it in his front jacket pocket. It was then Goldwater and the audience noticed my mike was unplugged from my recorder. He tossed the mike back on the stage behind him. A politician and a reporter have to roll with the punches.

But at that earlier visit and press conference, Goldwater spoke of the optimism he had for the 1980s. "For the young people in America, the future has never been so bright." He wished he would live for another 50 years, "because I think we're going to see mankind make more progress than he's made in the last seven thousand years." But he had a warning. "We definitely have all the makings of real trouble." He outlined the political scenario that, at that time, included the large Soviet Empire pitted against the Chinese as well as the Soviets engaged in a war in Afghanistan. He pointed to a trouble point in Yugoslavia and the uncertain future of that nation in 1980.

He also was concerned about the tension between Poland and the Soviet Union. Poland, he said, "just in effect told the Soviet Union to 'go to hell' and they had a general strike and they won. Now it doesn't appear that the Soviets are going to do anything about that." This was obviously before the breakup of the Soviet Union and perhaps Goldwater had a well-tuned eye on the future. He said at the time if the Soviets didn't do anything about the strike, "I wouldn't bet on it, but I can foresee other strikes in the general Warsaw Pact area. I think the Soviets are in a position probably weaker than they've ever been." He admitted he could be wrong, but he spoke with optimism when he saw what he called, "a better chance for a general period of peace than I've seen in a long time." Less than a dozen years later the Berlin Wall had come down, the Soviet Union had broken into lesser states and the Cold War was over. Barry Goldwater probably wasn't psychic, but perhaps one key to knowing the future is a keen understanding of the past and present.

A press conference including me with Cesar Chavez in Yuma, which was Chavez' hometown. Interestingly I was with Cesar on the Ides of March, March 15, 1981. I don't remember if I asked a question although I would do an interview in Stockton years later.

NIXON WAS MY FIRST BIG STORY. WAS IT GOOD FOR HIM TOO?

BEFORE I EVER got into radio, while still in college, my first real big-time reporter-type story, I guess you'd call it, was covering the arrival of President Richard Nixon in Phoenix, Arizona.

Richard Nixon in Phoenix from my 8mm movie camera

Presidential visits would always fascinate me. I was a journalism student at Mesa Community College in Mesa, (oddly enough) Arizona and I was writing the story for the school paper, then called the "Hokam Legend." That's Ho KAM, not hokum. It was Halloween 1970. Just the day before we had watched TV coverage of Nixon in San Jose, California standing on his limousine waving defiantly at the crowd. When he arrived at the Air National Guard Hangar in Phoenix, across the runways from Sky Harbor Airport, it was my first experience seeing history in the flesh. Of course, his flesh, or image anyway, became even larger than life, either in a good or bad way, depending on your view. My view was from near the back of the crowd. In the corner, to my left, (or port side) I could see a sign that read, "We don't want to know the way to San Jose," a play on the words to the Burt Bacharach song and an obvious pro-Nixon sign.

As a history buff, I was just as excited about seeing the plane that Nixon flew to Phoenix. It was a 707 jet, with the serial number 26000. Only a real trivia (there's fake trivia?) buff would appreciate that. I do hope you qualify. This is the same plane that John Kennedy took to Dallas and the plane Lyndon Johnson took the Oath of Office on and flew back to Washington. I suppose most people wouldn't care, but I find it "tres cool" as some might say in stuffy historical collecting jargon.

Okay, flashback to 1963. JFK has just been shot. I'm sitting in seventh grade class at Our Lady of Mount Carmel School in Tempe, Arizona, talking to my classmate and friend Terry. Tell me, is this an omen of a career in journalism or what? We're discussing what the headline would say that night about Kennedy. That's scary. Not the omen, but that I came that close to being a damn print journalist! You see, in all friendliness, I found a strange -- well, tension is not the exact word -- distance -- yeah, that'll work, between print and broadcast reporters. The print-types didn't think we were the reporters they were. Sometimes the public seemed to agree. Think of the times you've discussed the news and you talk about seeing it on television and reading it in the paper. Hearing it on the radio is sometimes a forgotten concept. Though I'll admit, I, too, sometimes had that "holier than thou" feeling when it's TV reporters versus radio, with me feeling we were more in the trenches than the blow dry set.

**The one time I got to appear on the cover of a magazine.
Okay it wasn't much, but it was a cover and it was a publication**

I ALWAYS CARRIED MY CAMERA.
AFTER ALL, THIS WAS RADIO

PRESIDENT RONALD REAGAN never made it to Yuma, at least while I was there, but I was able to see The Gipper for the first time at a Phoenix airport departure in 1982. Reagan was leaving after consoling Nancy Reagan's mother after the death of her husband, Nancy's father, in Phoenix. This presidential departure point was again the Air Guard Hangar across the runways from Phoenix Sky Harbor Airport. It was my second presidential appearance and the same location as the 1970 Nixon event. Organizers had a flatbed trailer for those of us in the local press to stand on, a good distance from the 707 jet parked there. Once again, as a history buff, to my excitement, I was glad to see aircraft 26000, the jet that JFK had taken to Dallas in 1963.

Ronald Reagan leaving Phoenix on historic aircraft SAM 26000

Before we were allowed on the press flatbed trailer, a dog sniffed it out. A security person also clicked off a frame on my camera and rolled the tape recorder to make sure it was a recorder. When the motorcade with Reagan arrived I was taking pictures for me and recording ambient sound of the jet whine for the radio report later. There's not much you can report when all a president does is drive up and climb up the ramp and wave goodbye. But you take what you can get, including the jet whine. I was actually able to put together a description I used on-air back at KAWC in Yuma. By this time I had switched from commercial stations KVOY/KJOK to KAWC, Yuma's NPR station at Arizona Western College.

This presidential visit to Phoenix also gave me firsthand knowledge of how the White House Press gets the breaks. That group was right up next to the plane. We locals were many yards away. There's another reason why a president can get isolated if it's almost always the same reporters asking questions, regardless where he goes.

As near as I can tell, this car that brought Reagan to the Air Guard hanger across from Sky Harbor Airport is the same one that was parked outside the Washington Hilton that Reagan was heading to on March 30, 1981 when John Hinckley shot him and three others. That car is now at the Henry Ford Museum in Dearborn, Michigan.

Another perk as a member of the media we got to learn from the Marine Corps Drill Team at Marine Corps Air Station, or MCAS Yuma, how to twirl a rifle. That bayonet was real. It was not without risk, but I did keep all my toes. I think of that as a victory.

As I've said several times, the best part of radio is the variety. How many other jobs let you take rifle-tossing lessons from the Marines (without having to enlist) or drive in a media stock car race? (I think I came in last, driving a Pinto numbered 00. Well, it was my first time and unlike one of my fellow media drivers, I, mind you, did not have to apologize for denting the borrowed race car.)

Fictional character Walter Mitty should have been a reporter. Did he ever get to take part in the Pachyderm 500 Elephant Race? I think not. But I did. I'm in the back in the light colored shirt. Of course it was only in a store parking lot and my elephant did link onto the tail of the one ahead of him so there wasn't much challenge. (I assume the elephant I rode was a "he" but it's difficult to turn an elephant over to check. I do love that joke.) The one I rode, at least, had short bristly hair. I cannot speak for all elephants.

When the Army's Golden Knights parachute team came to Yuma I got to ride up with them, and ride down without them. In those days at least, they were flying in a Hercules C-130 for their jumps.

The only way I could tell I was in flight was when the air got colder or I could look out that little round hole. Oh I know it's a porthole, I'm just kidding. Give me some credit. I know all about aviation and boating terms. I know all about running upstairs and downstairs on some boat and then from the back to the stern! (yeah, I know, I know, no nautical letters please. I would rather knot. Boy they just keep coming, don't they?) Anyway, flying in the C-130 is like riding in the belly of a whale, with fewer teeth, of course and no stomach bile. Okay, it's a gross analogy.

With the Golden Knights and their C-130 Hercules 1984

I did know we were several thousand feet up, though, when the rear hatch opened. As you may know, that's the hatch they open to drive equipment in and out of the back of the plane. All the jumpers in yellow jumpsuits left that way. The rest of us came down the easy way.

**Above Yuma, Arizona looking through the open back end of the
Golden Knights C-130 Hercules**

When I was in Yuma and probably still, Yuma and the military were synonymous. The Marine Corps Air Station Yuma was next to the Yuma International Airport and the Marines operated the control tower for both. The city had its big military appreciation days called MAD. That stood for, well, Military Appreciation Days. The Golden Knights would come for the festivities and so would the Blue Angels as they stopped on their national tour. Of course, the Blue Angels are a flying recruitment poster for the Navy but it's still fun to watch these pilots. They've changed planes over the years that included the A-4 Skyhawk they flew while I was in Yuma, but the precision is still stunning, as you know if you've seen them.

Talking to the pilots was easy too, as they were friendly and articulate, with full answers. However, the shortest answer I got was from then-Lieutenant Curt Watson. It came shortly after the Air Force Thunderbirds tragedy, when the jets, flying as a group, crashed in the desert, following their lead plane right into the ground. First, I asked Watson if there were any jealousies between the Blue Angels and the Thunderbirds. He said there was some friendly poking of fun, but they helped each other whenever they could. A few moments later I asked him if the major accident had any dramatic psychological effect on the team. "No," he answered. "Really?" I said. "Not at all" responded Watson, in a less than elaborate answer. That was probably intentional. As the public relations arm of the Navy, I understand why it appeared to me he took a hard bank to steer clear of any elaboration.

One actor to visit Yuma seemed to have a lot of respect for the military. Enough anyway to make the Marines the central theme of his new TV show. Robert Conrad brought his film crew to Marine Corps Air

Station Yuma, giving me up close and personal access to him and his film production process.

ROBERT CONRAD

I'm 48 years old and movin'. I don't get the Travolta letters and I don't want 'em."

RED WEST

"This arm won't straighten out from falling on it so many times. This scar here was made by a piano that was supposed to break away and my head broke away instead. But it was fun. Pay was good."

Actor Robert Conrad was born in Chicago in 1935 and left us in 2020 at age 84, but when we talked in 1983, his life had improved with age. He was filming the pilot episode of a show called "Hard Knox" where his character, Joe Knox, was about to head a military academy. I actually found a DVD with the pilot episode, so to speak. Conrad was filming on the Marine Base in Yuma. He expected "Hard Knox" to be more fun than "Wild, Wild West," the famous show from the 1960s where characters Jim West and Artemus Gordon were Secret Service agents in the 1800s. When he was doing "Wild, Wild West," Conrad, as Agent Jim West, was in his 20s. But that was past and he told me he had no interest in going back in time. "I have more things to enjoy now than I had when I was in my 20s, you know? I enjoy the liquor more, I enjoy my wife more, I enjoy my grandson, I enjoy work more. I mean, I'm havin' a good time, contrary to anything you might think," he laughed. "I'm havin' fun."

I pointed out I thought there were several people working with him on this series who had worked with him on "Baa Baa Black Sheep" and I asked if it were enjoyable to surround himself with people with whom he had previously worked. I don't know if he took a bit of offense at that but he told me he didn't "surround" himself with people and the choice of who works with him was not a personality contest. "I hire people by their ability." He said, "if they can't cut it they don't work for me."

Conrad told me "Hard Knox" was the first time he had financial responsibility for a show. "I've had control before. It's one thing when you're responsible for something like this. It's another thing when you're financially damaged. It took us two hours today to get a sequence that will last 30 seconds. That cost me, our company, $20,000, but it was worth it." Conrad was hoping the show would "go into profit" as he put it, about the fourth or fifth episode. At the time of our interview the show was "in deficit," but he said, "that's the name of the game, you know? It's why I drink a lot of margaritas, I think." Unfortunately I don't think the series got beyond this pilot episode. But Conrad had a long resume going into "Hard Knox" and he had a lengthy career. His credits in his long life in show biz include everything from a "Maverick" episode in 1959 to "Mission Impossible" to, of course, "Wild, Wild West," as well as playing Major Greg "Pappy" Boyington in "Baa Baa Black Sheep," about a World War Two fighter squadron.

In the 1970s Conrad starred in the TV series, "The D. A." He also portrayed G. Gordon Liddy in the Liddy biography, "Will." In 1996 Conrad appeared in the movie, "Jingle All The Way" and in 1999 had a guest appearance in the TV show, "Just Shoot Me" and worked with Kelsey Grammer in the movie, "New Jersey Turnpikes." He also appeared on an episode of "Nash Bridges" in 2000. In our 1980s interview I asked if he were getting into any kind of movie work or if television was his medium. He told me of his role as a general the year before in a movie with Sean Connery called "Wrong Is Right." "I am really more interested in acting and producing." He liked being around the problems that you have to deal with. "I like to see young people play roles and be good in it. I get a personal satisfaction out of that." Conrad enjoyed seeing Red West, his friend, at that time, of 26 years, grow as an actor. Red West's career included work as an actor, stuntman and former Elvis Presley associate. Now that's a resume you don't see everyday! Red West was also playing a role in this show as he had in "Baa Baa Black Sheep." When we talked in '83, Conrad said his buddy's part in "Hard Knox" was probably one of Red's proudest moments. "He is a former Marine and to be here playing this role," said Conrad, "is something that I think is worth more to Red than money."

Conrad told a story he felt was a good example of the type of relationship between him and Red West. Conrad was on the Marine base in Yuma and had to "use the head" or in civilian terms, the restroom. Conrad said, "one (entrance) said 'Officers' and one said 'Enlisted Men'...I said 'Red, let's hit the head together and he said 'okay.' I walked in and came out (of the officer's restroom) and I said, 'What happened to Red?' Well, he went to where he naturally wanted to be, (the) enlisted man's head." Conrad laughed when he said, "that seems to be our relationship for 26 years."

Conrad planned to integrate some episodes of the show with the Marine Corps, such as the Marine Corps birthday on November 10. Conrad added, "once a Marine always a Marine, except for (Lee Harvey) Oswald, right?"

I asked him if he hoped people looked on him differently after the role in "Hard Knox." He quickly answered, "I don't care how people look on me." So I asked how he felt about the opinion of professional people? "I'm not that vain. I mean, I do the very damndest I can, the best I can, and I walk away from it. I'm not real humble but I'm very modest in a lot of peculiar ways."

In 1983 he felt he had the ability to pretty much pick and choose the parts he wanted to do. He said, "yeah, I'd have to say if this were military, because Yuma is a military town, I'm about a two star in real life, movin' for four," he said, laughing.

ROBERT GENE "RED" **West's days as** Elvis Presley's associate and as a songwriter for Elvis were long behind him in 1983 when we met at Marine Corps Air Station Yuma on the location set of "Hard Knox." West said his decades-long relationship with Robert Conrad began with a game of touch football in a park at Beverly Glen and Sunset. West worked as a stuntman on "Wild, Wild West" on almost all of the episodes, but he had an acting role on "Baa Baa Black Sheep" as Sergeant Andy Micklin. His other credits also include a role on "Will" with Conrad. West was a party guest in "Blue Hawaii" as well as playing a part in "The Legend of Grizzly Adams" in 1990, an ice cream vendor in the movie, "Clambake" with Elvis Presley and James Gregory and the role of Sheriff Tanner in "Walking Tall. His show business resume also included the role of Red Webster in "Road House" in 1989 and a judge in the Oliver Stone film, "Natural Born Killers" in 1990. His list includes the character of Paulsen in "I Still Know What You Did Last Summer" in 1998 and work in "Cookie's Fortune" in 1999. I pointed out stunt work in the 1960s TV show "Wild, Wild West" must have kept him in most of the scenes. "Kept me in most of the hospitals too." He said they were crazy in those days but he stopped in mid sentence. "Well we're still nuts, but in those days Bob (Conrad) had a fractured skull and numerous injuries and this arm won't straighten out from falling on it so many times, and this scar here was made by a piano that was supposed to break away and my head broke away instead. But it was fun. Pay was good and I enjoyed it, I really did."

He figured he'd take a role in front of the camera for "Hard Knox" as Red Tuttle, the maintenance chief, similar to what he played in "Baa Baa Black Sheep." Being on camera has its advantages. He laughed when he said, "it's a lot safer here." By this time West had backed off the stunt work. In "Magnum, P.I." West said he "had to do a small fight scene and go through a wall, "nothin' real hairy like no more horse falls or car crashes...I let the guys that do that for a living do it. I'm outta that line of work." He said he no longer had a tendency to keep taking falls. West said, "no, I'm too old for that. I hate to say that but I let the younger men do that now."

Yuma's ability to bring fascinating celebrities to town was certainly enhanced by the work of Arizona Western College. One such performer was a man who could amaze you. Hence the title, "The Amazing Kreskin." Is it an act or a stunning display of mental awareness? Probably depends on whom you ask. Fortunately, I talked to Kreskin.

KRESKIN

"We slammed the door of the safe and I had to try to open the safe. There was only one problem. The only person who could think of the combination, who knew it, was the man who was inside the safe with 15 minutes air."

He calls himself a mentalist, an entertainer, but "The Amazing Kreskin" would also tell you straight out he couldn't see the future or read minds and he didn't have any supernatural powers. He made a career of picking up on people's thoughts and influencing them. Though an entertainer, he said he took his work as a mentalist seriously and noted there have been people in all cultures who seemed to be able to sense or feel thoughts of others. When we talked in 1982 he told me he never understood why more of the prophets or soothsayers didn't spend more time at the racetracks. So I asked, how about him? "That's interesting you ask me. I've only gone to a racetrack twice in my life. I just don't know much about horseracing." The first time he went was with a doctor friend and a priest. Kreskin told me he said at the time, "well you'd better place the bets for me because if people see me betting, they're gonna bet on the horses I'm betting on and I don't want people to lose all their money." He played all of the races, "and I won all but one race, and I was just guessing." I asked if he could help us out next time he was in town. Kreskin told me, "I don't read the minds of horses, Biff."

In the early '80s he was concerned over something that you might say is still a problem decades later. "There's a plethora of interest in so-called psychic phenomena. There are people who are now, not simply claiming to advise people of their lives, of their futures, but they're claiming to heal and all of these." He says people who will go to someone, regardless of their claims, who say or imply they will change their lives, have one of four problems. He includes money, love life, job or future, and health. When a desperate person gets a suggestion for their future or something to avoid or a danger, Kreskin says, "that prophecy can be self fulfilling because of the person dwelling on it so greatly and I don't want to encourage this area. That's why I discount and discard so many areas."

Kreskin pointed out his show did not include putting anyone in a trance. He didn't believe hypnotic trances existed. "It is simply, Biff, a figment of the imagination." Kreskin said, "I don't care what the medical hypnotist says. I don't really care what the psychiatrist says. I think they'd better face the fact they're probably the only ones that are being hypnotized, not their patient or subject." He said he could create the same response to the power of suggestion without any trance. Kreskin added, "if we realize the power of suggestion, Biff, it'll shed much greater light on the nature of riots, the nature of some of the cult groups, why certain charismatic figures all through history have had an influence over us." He said it may also show what was meant by all of the positive thinking books of the 1930s through the 1970s, "where they suggested if you think of something strongly enough you tend to make it happen. The real answer is within ourselves, and that tool starts with the imagination."

I wondered if there were other applications for his talent, other than stage shows. "As a thought reader in my everyday life, of course I don't. I'd be a nervous wreck if I were trying to pick up people's feelings, ideas." He said the real use of his field is in the area of the power of suggestion and ideas.

Kreskin and his talent had been at the job since he was eleven, as a living, and before that he was practicing at the age of five, six, seven years old. William Shatner, of "Star Trek" fame, was on Kreskin's show and once told him that kids understood the terminology of his ability, such as telepathy. When Kreskin was young, children didn't think too much of those terms. But Shatner reminded Kreskin that when they were kids, there wasn't a series called "Star Trek." Kreskin said, "many themes of that science fiction series had some of the phenomena that I was involved in."

He recalled one of his most dramatic moments on his TV series. He said a man had enough confidence in him to climb into a safe. The safe was small enough that the subject had to crouch. "We slammed the door of the safe and I had to try to open the safe. There was only one problem. The only person who could think of the combination, who knew it, was the man who was inside the safe with 15 minutes air." Kreskin took more than 12 minutes to free the man. Kreskin said it was "scary." I don't know if he tried it after we met.

One appearance not so scary was on "The Tonight Show" when Johnny Carson was host. I remembered it and asked him about the time a table flew around the stage. "That was not magic. People were resting their hands on tables, sitting in circles...four at a table, and they were concentrating and the tables started to rattle and shake and move and it was through the concentration of people and their nervous energy and reactions, as surprising as it may seem. There was enough interaction of unconscious activity...through their physical nervous system, that reactions were taking place in the table." Kreskin said one table, a card table, flipped over in mid-air and ran into Carson's desk. During the commercial break, "one of the men...went over to Carson and said, 'gee, I'd like to buy that table,' and it was a riotous request because the table wasn't the key. It was how I got them to concentrate."

You might have noticed I keep referring to Kreskin as just that, Kreskin. That's because he legally changed it to just the one name. That may work on stage but his road manager explained to me the airlines didn't take it in stride. Seems they needed an initial to go with that last name. The manager showed me Kreskin's plane ticket. It read T. A. Kreskin with the T. A. standing for, of course, "The Amazing." The local college contact for his appearance, as well as Kreskin, his road manager and I went out to dinner after the show and I had him sign his book for me. He produced a clever way of inscribing a book, "ESPecially, Kreskin." I had him add something to mine. He wrote a nice note in the book, signing it ESPecially, (and at my insistence) T. A. Kreskin. That could a one of a kind signature.

If you want to interview fascinating people or even figures from history, sometimes all you have to do is make a local call. Jerald Agenbroad was present at a political assassination and even wounded in the attack. He was also just down the road at the Marine base.

JERALD AGENBROAD

"The fellow from the front of the truck was beginning to get out of the truck and started a broken field, football-type run over towards where Sadat was seated, and just about simultaneously then, the three agents from

the back of the truck opened up on the crowd, and just in the general area with automatic weapon fire."

When I met Marine Lieutenant Colonel Jerald Agenbroad, it had been two and a half years since the military and fluke of chance had put him in the middle of one of the most historic events in modern Middle East history, the assassination of Egyptian President Anwar Sadat. On October 6, 1981, Agenbroad was with the Rapid Deployment Joint Task Force as the aide to the commander. The general had been invited to a parade planned in Cairo to commemorate the start of the Yom Kippur War of 1967. Where the general goes, so goes his aide and that put Agenbroad in the parade reviewing stands. He said it was "an invitation I couldn't turn down...Poor choice of invitations to accept I guess." Also in the stands, but of course with a front row seat, was Anwar Sadat.

Agenbroad arrived at the stands about a half-hour before Sadat got there and the parade started almost immediately after that. Agenbroad said, "it was a rather lengthy parade. I would say the parade at the time of the assassination attempt had been going on for probably an hour and a half or close to two hours." He remembered it as a really pretty day, in an area where the sun shines a lot and there's a lot of blue sky. Agenbroad didn't have any feeling of pending disaster. "As far as we knew everything was peaceful. This particular event came as a total surprise to everybody, I think, except the perpetrators."

He had not met Sadat, but Agenbroad noticed that just looking at him you could pick him out of a crowd as a very impressive sort of person. He said Sadat was watching a unique military parade. "Most of the way through the parade they had something going on in the air overhead, as well as something on the ground. It was at the latter stages of the parade...There were two separate groups of airplanes putting on an air show overhead," and there were trucks pulling artillery pieces on the ground. "There was a flight of six Mirages making a low pass from out of view behind us, to in view in front of us, and as everybody was watching the airplanes go by, an explosion took place that directed everybody's attention back down in front, and what we saw...was that one of the trucks which was pulling the artillery piece was in the final stages of coming to a stop, directly in front of where President Sadat was sitting."

Agenbroad said, "there was a puff of smoke about halfway between the truck and the stands." That puff of smoke was from a grenade "which had been thrown from the truck over to where Sadat was and had hit a wall in front of Sadat, ricocheted back towards the truck and exploded about halfway between the two. At the same time, the fellow from the front of the truck was beginning to get out of the truck and started a broken field, football-type run over towards where Sadat was seated and just about simultaneously then, the three agents from the back of the truck opened up on the crowd and just in the general area with automatic weapon fire." Agenbroad said they "continued to do that for some matter of seconds until the fellow that had gotten out of the front of the truck was able to get over to where Sadat was." Agenbroad found it hard to sort out all the little details, "but almost immediately then (that shooter) was able to sort of reach over the wall in front of Sadat and fire his gun down into the area where Sadat was on the ground."

Agenbroad took a bullet in the leg, "probably in the first four or five seconds. When the three (men) from the back of the truck were firing at the crowd that's when myself and the fellow sitting next to me both were shot." Agenbroad didn't think the other shooters were targeting anyone specifically. "I think they had some general assigned areas for fire, but I think it was not aimed directly at me or any other specific person. It was just fire designed to keep any return fire from coming back and interfering with the assassination attempt."

Agenbroad said it was hard to say exactly when President Sadat was struck. He said, "(Sadat's) initial reaction was to stand up when the assassination began. It's not an impossibility that he was shot at that time. They immediately then pulled him back down and I think nobody can swear to the fact that he was intact at that time." The entire event was over pretty quickly. As he pointed out, "I would say that the beginning to end was probably less than 30 seconds."

There was speculation the Egyptian president stood in defiance as the assassination began. Agenbroad didn't see Sadat stand but also didn't think the president was showing defiance. "You've got to put this in context a little bit and remember that it was just a routine military parade and to say that a person could, in that length of time, which is virtually no time at all, make the transition from a routine celebration-type military parade to an assassination attempt; we certainly didn't make that transition mentally that quickly." He said it "took some seconds to figure out exactly what was going on, and the initial reaction could have been one of more puzzlement rather than an accurate analysis instantly that that's what was happening."

Agenbroad admitted his perceptions about the crowd after the shootings may not have been totally accurate, but he didn't remember people at the beginning running around shouting. Was the crowd composed? He said there was puzzlement with people trying to figure out what was going on. "I don't know if composed is the word but let's say frozen into inactivity for a moment, because it was really quick. The whole thing was over very quick." He added it wasn't a mass exit scene, "like you see in the soccer games and people get crushed and pushed. People just weren't moving initially."

The response by Egyptian emergency personnel impressed Agenbroad. He said this was cetainly not something they expected to have happen and immediatedly they had to deal with mass casualties. Agenbroad was among the lesser wounded, and he said he was on the way to the hospital. within about 20 minutes, adding, "so I think they did a pretty remarkable job of getting the thing sorted out and evacuated in an orderly fashion." Agenbroad's leg was severely damaged in the 1981 attack, but that was his only injury. When we talked in 1983 he still had a limp but he expected to fully recover.

Given the choice, he would not have participated in that moment of history, but he described it as "interesting." He said he was more of an observer than an "active participant." That kind of event could make someone think twice about ever attending another parade, but Agenbroad wasn't scared off. "As far as paranoia about parades, we say that in jest, but no, not really." As far as attitudes toward life, Agenbroad talked with others who faced trauma and had come close to death and he said it gave him a different perspective on life, one of more tolerance and "an appreciation for the small things that probably you didn't have before."

After Sadat was killed by Islamic fundamentalists from his own military, Hosni Mubarek took over the presidency. Decades later, Mubarek lost his power. The region continues to struggle with the issue of peace but that one dark moment of violence caught up Jerald Agenbroad.

THE RUSSIANS WERE SAFER THAN THEY THOUGHT. IF THEY ONLY KNEW

AS A LIBERTARIAN, it was a bit ironic for me to work at a state-owned radio station. KAWC in Yuma was the NPR member station at Arizona Western College. About the only way I can justify it in my mind is to think that I was recouping, in salary, all the taxes I felt I should not have had to pay over the years. I'm aware that argument's a bit thin, but it'll have to do. KAWC (That's K-Arizona Western College. Remember, stations like doing that) was a community AM only station but in those days, it was also a training ground for broadcasting students. One of my favorite memories of the students is the time the program log, the document that says what you should be playing on the air at any given time, called for an Emergency Broadcast Systems Test. You know, "this is a test. It is only a test," that in those days was followed by a long, high pitched tone. I'm of the opinion an emergency alert should also include something like 'had this been an actual alert, this station would have shut down and all personnel would be long gone before this tone ended," or words to that effect. Anyway, one day I walked into the main control room. The student on the air was sitting at the control board. Phil (his real name) was making a sound, a long sound, a real long vocal ooooooooooooooooooooooooooooo! Seems Phil couldn't find the tape that had the recorded tone on it. He became a human EBS warning tone. Who says college students aren't resourceful?

Speaking of broadcasting education, I suppose it's valuable training for the college students to learn how to do a lengthy sporting event from numerous broadcast vantage points. That must have been the thinking, but who would want to listen to an all-day bicycle race, on the radio? We broadcast it, though, at Arizona Western College. The circular drive around the campus was the track. We had students stationed around the course, with one even on a "cherry picker" high up with a wireless mike. How many times can you say, "here they come again?" I mean, you don't even get sound effects from a bicycle. There's no roar of the greasepaint, no smell of the crowd. Maybe we should have put playing cards in the bicycle spokes. I think we mostly taught the students if you want to be in radio, you must do pointless things.

As news producer and host and producer of a station talk show I was looking for a variety of guests. Another celebrity fell into my lap. Though Jan Berry of Jan and Dean was in town, when we tried to set up the interview he was sleeping and apparently wasn't too anxious to wake up, so I was afraid an interview wouldn't happen. It did, though, as local TV host Gracie Hammons, as well as another radio show host, Pat Maestro, who specialized in oldies and I gathered at Jan's motel to each conduct our interviews.

JAN BERRY

"The recording is called 'Dead Man's Curve." It was kind of an omen."

In 1965 singers Jan Berry and Dean Torrence were at the top of their game. Jan and Dean had met the "Little Old Lady from Pasadena," conquered "Surf City" and gone "Sidewalk Surfin'." In 1966, Jan Berry was nearly killed, not on "Dead Man's Curve," but in a real life car crash. He told me the song "Dead Man's Curve" was his favorite because he saw it as "kind of an omen, so to speak." He says it was a weird song but "a good sound," with lyrics about racing and good times and Hollywood. "That was a good time and it was lots of fun. It was just another song, but it was good."

After Jan Berry's car crash, the song did appear to have been something of an omen. It's all the more ironic when you listen to Berry's introduction to the song at a 1960s concert in Sacramento, California. In that album you can hear Jan Berry tell the audience they wanted to do a song about a place in front of Dean's driveway. Jan joked that Dean wasn't a very good driver when he came home late at night and had trouble making it into his driveway, so Jan told the audience they nicknamed the spot, "Dead Man's Curve." As it turned out the danger lay in wait for Jan. In our talk in 1984, Jan still suffered the effects of the crash 18 years earlier. He spoke haltingly, was partially disabled and had difficulty walking. But he was still performing and in the time we spent together was as mellow and as pleasant as you could want.

It must have been a heady thrill at one time to have thousands of screaming teenagers at concerts and Berry agreed, calling it "nifty." Berry says the accident added a little complication to his performing, but he says, "I'll tell you, I'm just playing and trying my best."

Brian Wilson of the Beach Boys collaborated with Jan and Dean on several of the duo's songs including "Surf City," "I Get Around," "Little Honda," and "Sidewalk Surfin'." In 1984, I asked Jan why he thought his music was still so popular. "Maybe like you said, we had a few hits." He also credits the surf craze and the Beach Boys. He said, "today they will still perform, and so Jan and Dean will do the same." Though the two groups went their separate ways, Berry said at the time, "we always get back and say hi to the Beach Boys and so it's just a good feeling."

When Jan and Dean were together, Jan said he never considered going out as a solo act.

Berry hoped to be an inspiration to the disabled. I asked if he were different emotionally after the accident. At that time it had been nearly 20 years since the crash, and as Berry said, everyone will "get, I don't like to call them old, but wiser, so to speak. But you may remember the times, but you will just keep moving on." He mentioned the complications and all the added music technology, but Berry said in 1984 the surfin' craze would still be there and one of the most famous residents of Surf City planned to keep rockin' and rollin' for a long time. He did that, too, until his death in 2004 at age 62.

Another man who felt he could make a difference for the disabled was Ken Jacuzzi. You know his name because you've seen it in bathhouses and maybe by your backyard pool. He was in Yuma too, not to perform, but to further his business ventures.

KEN JACUZZI

"If you mention the name Jacuzzi, everybody automatically thinks you're extremely wealthy...It can really be a detriment to making an economical purchase at times."

Imagine going into pool and exercise areas nearly anywhere and seeing your name next to the whirlpool. Ken Jacuzzi, of Jacuzzi whirlpool fame, admitted it was a kick for him to see his name. The Jacuzzi family sold the business in the late 1970s but that doesn't always matter if there's public name recognition. He said, "I often think when I'm going out to purchase something that -- as a matter of fact I have done it a couple of times -- used my wife's maiden name, because in certain circumstances if you mention the name Jacuzzi, everybody automatically thinks you're extremely wealthy. In my case, although I'm well off, I'm not extremely wealthy and it can really be a detriment to making an economical purchase at times."

When we talked in 1983, Ken Jacuzzi used a wheelchair, As a child he suffered from rheumatoid arthritis and it was his father who recognized the value of home hydrotherapy for his son. That was the birth of the home whirlpool bath. Jacuzzi remembered "when I was about seven or eight years old, my doctor prescribed hydrotherapy treatments at the local children's hospital in Oakland, California, and I was taken there by my parents several times a week." They noticed some improvement in his range of motion. Jacuzzi said, "since the family was in the pump business and my dad knew what the hydrotherapy device looked like and how it performed, he thought I could benefit from hydrotherapy treatments at home on a daily basis...so he developed a unit for the home bathtub." When it was shown to his doctor, the doctor suggested Ken Jacuzzi's father build and sell them to people for home treatment. I didn't think to ask Jacuzzi if the doctor got a cut of the profits.

The Jacuzzi name was closely tied to the product and the company fought for years to keep the name from becoming generic. "People at Coca-Cola or Xerox, Kleenex, did a little bit better job than we did in defending their proprietary names." He added Jacuzzi was used quite often "as a generic name meaning whirlpool baths."

It took many years for us to meet, but finally I got the chance to tell Mr. Jacuzzi how his name had been so closely tied to mine. When people heard Jannuzzi, often I would hear, "Oh, like Jacuzzi." Everyone who said that always thought they were the first to have that thought. I told Ken Jacuzzi his name had been around me for a long time. Jacuzzi (not Jannuzzi) said, "I can imagine, yes."

Ken Jacuzzi saw himself as a trailblazer with a product known worldwide. He said, "I think one of the first times I noticed the whirlpool type products mentioned in a major work of literature was in George Orwell's novel "1984."" Jacuzzi noted, "certainly he alludes to those kinds of products being very popular and as a matter of fact they are and we're nearly at 1984." When we talked Jacuzzi's software company had just been developed to produce high quality educational software aimed at adults. He predicted the new trends in invention and developing would be in computers and health care. He also saw the banking industry getting more involved in computers and predicted in 1983 that the day of home banking with a personal computer was very close. Turns out he was right.

Jacuzzi was also involved with the Arthritis Foundation, the Easter Seals Society and United Cerebral Palsy. He had some advice that's probably still timely. He urged someone with a handicap to not let it keep them from making a difference. "Today the opportunities are much greater for a handicapped person than they were 30 years ago, 25 years ago, 20 years ago. There's been a great deal of improvement with respect to eliminating architectural barriers and that sort of thing." And his comments came before the Americans With Disabilities Act. He felt the educational opportunities had become much greater, as well as employment opportunities, though he said there were still some big difficulties. But he said, "the only way to overcome your handicap is just go out and do what you like doing and do it as well as you can." Ken Jacuzzi spent part of his life working for the disabled in Arizona as director of the Office of the Americans with Disabilities.

He died in 2017 at age 75.

WILLIE TYLER AND LESTER

"They'll Accept It From Him More So Than They Would Me"

Sure, I've interviewed dummies. One time it was true in a somewhat different way. Remember Willie Tyler and Lester? Both had what then were called "Afro" haircuts. Lester, (the dummy) wore a little British sports cap and a sleeveless sweater, which is odd, because how cold can a dummy get? But then, if the dummy got cold and he didn't bring the sweater, well, then he'd really be a dummy, wouldn't he? I'm almost sure I'm right on that.

One real problem with a wooden interviewee, (I don't mean Al Gore) is that I didn't know where to point the microphone.

Willie (the real guy) told me Lester was the extrovert while he was the introvert. Lester (the dummy -- stay with me here) says things Willie couldn't get away with. He (Willie, not Lester...I think) said, "they'll accept it from him more so than they would me, because he's like a little elf, if you will. They think he's a real personality and that's great." Willie said people in airports would say to him, 'Where's Lester?' "It's not like, 'how are you doin', Willie?'" At that time, Willie said they were marketing t-shirts with Lester's face, adding, "if they put me on the T-shirt, nobody knows who I am." Lester chimed in with, "yeah, I love it and it makes me feel real." At least I think it was Lester. It's hard to know what's real.

Willie said he had to believe Lester was real, but that belief never crossed that same line Anthony Hopkins crossed in the movie "Magic." However, Willie did tell the story of a ventriloquist who shared a dressing room with a singer. The ventriloquist was doing his act and the shoe came off the dummy while on stage, knocking a glass over on some customers. Later when the singer came back to their shared dressing room, she knocked on the door and heard two people arguing. Unfortunately for the sanity of the ventriloquist, there was only one person in the room -- the ventriloquist -- and then there was the dummy he was reprimanding. Willie says, "that's in the gray area." Yes, indeed!

Joyce Brothers is one person who was probably used to working with people who fall into gray areas. The celebrity psychiatrist was in Yuma, sponsored by the local hospice organization. Another reporter, Kim Johnson and I, talked to her at the Yuma Airport lobby, a place that became an easy meeting ground for press and famous folks passing through.

JOYCE BROTHERS

"On 'Family Feud' they asked, 'who are the ten greatest intellects living or dead?' and I'm on the list along with Kissinger and that just surprised me. One wonders about the audience, but...I'm pleased to be on the list."

Doctor Joyce Brothers liked the kidding and the nice comments she got. At least that was her attitude when we talked in 1983. Maybe the "Psychologist Extraordinaire" as she was once described, changed later in life, but when she talked with us in the Yuma airport Brothers said even a description as a "pop psychologist" pleased her. As she put it, "I think it's important that people are able to get information that you can get across to people what we know about behavior at this point, in the popular literature, in the popular media."

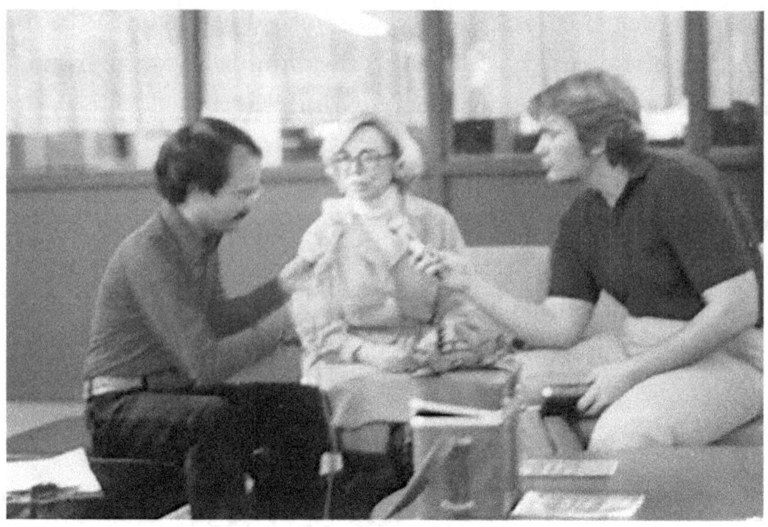

Brothers was asked how appearing in everything from game shows to "Happy Days" tied into helping people relate to their lives. She said sometimes she did things just for the fun of it, adding, "I think psychologists have a right to have fun too." But she said, "sometimes it's a way of getting a little piece of information across to a lot of people." Brothers used soap operas to talk to young people about the dangers of the drug PCP. She would see college students watching soaps and knew they could get the information in a way that was meaningful to them. Brothers quoted the saying, "the mind absorbs what the seat endures" and with millions of people watching you can get across a lot of information.

Brothers also spoke about aging and pointed out it's been shown that getting older doesn't mean the loss of mental ability. She cited tests that show I.Q. will increase as you age if you keep challenging your mind and continue to learn.

The noted psychologist said getting older we sort out what's important and emotional life improves. "We get, not older and more crotchety, but rather we get older and nicer. We get along better with people as we get older. We get to understand people better as we get older, so while we may lose some of the sight and some of the hearing we more than make up for it."

When you think of Joyce Brothers, you probably don't think of boxing. It's not a logical mental leap. But boxing and her knowledge of it helped her win big on the 1950s game show "$64,000 Question." That show was also in the middle of the game show scandals but Brothers was cleared of any wrongdoing. She once even co-hosted a show called "Sports Showcase," but boxing, when we talked in 1983, was not a big interest for her.

Game shows remain popular and gambling seems to have increased across the country -- at least the legal side of it. Brothers said at the time, "there are a great many people who gamble a small amount of money, what they can afford, and they get entertainment out of it. For the person who has a very controlled life they get a chance to be uncontrolled, for the moment. For the person who has a dull life they have a chance to get a little bit of excitement, for the moment. For the person whose boss always tells him or her what to do, they have a chance to be their own boss for that moment." She said if it's used for entertainment that's fine, but Brothers warns it can be abused. "If money is spent that should be money that children should have for food, and there are gamblers who will spend that money, there is an addiction to gambling. So I think it can be fine for most people but it can be a trap for some."

Brothers arrived at Yuma International Airport in February wearing snow boots. They looked out of place in sunny Arizona, but not in the snow covered East where her flight began. One bystander came up and asked to see the boots. Brothers laughed when she told him the boots were from New York. She explained she was wearing boots because "our method of snow removal in New York is called July."

An airport is also a good and logical place to talk with a pilot. Although in this case we were on the Marine base side of the jointly-operated Yuma airport and standing near the flight line. The setting might have been unusual for the other reporter and me, but probably felt like home to stunt pilot Art Scholl.

ART SCHOLL

"They said, 'well, he's the highest paid guy in Hollywood but he's the only one left alive'… and I thought, well, you know, I've been doing this for quite a few years and I did look back and yes, all our other stunt pilots have been killed."

One thing Art Scholl took very seriously was safety. It made his death all the more ironic. The stunt pilot and actor was not a lightweight in the field. Scholl held a Bachelors, Masters and Doctorate in aeronautical engineering. In September 1985, Scholl was filming background for the Tom Cruise movie "Top Gun" off the coast of California near Carlsbad. He was doing an inverted flat spin in a biplane with a camera mounted in front. About 1,500 feet Scholl radioed "I have a problem" and then "I really have a problem." Scholl and the plane hit the water and sunk in the ocean, killing Scholl.. The movie "Top Gun" was dedicated to Scholl, who, when he died at age 54, left an impressive resume. His TV stunt or feature appearances included "Baa Baa Black Sheep," "The A Team," "Fantasy Island," "CHIPS," and others. In the movies you might have seen Scholl or his stunt work in "Blue Thunder," "The Right Stuff," "Indiana Jones and the Temple of Doom" and appropriately, "The Art Scholl Story" to name just some of his credits.

Even if you never saw Scholl on film you could have seen him in person. He was a featured air show performer with ratings in helicopters, gliders, single and multi-engine planes, as well as being a flight instructor. For air shows, Scholl had two modified Pennzoil Chipmunks. The plane was the post war Royal Canadian Air Force basic trainer and Scholl modified the wings and changed the engine to give a cruise speed of 165 miles an hour. Two of his maneuvers included the Lomcevak, which is a climb straight up and a controlled fall, as well as his inverted ribbon pickup where he would fly upside down and pick up a horizontal ribbon strung just a few feet above the ground.

It was at an air show just a year and half before his deadly crash that another reporter and I had the opportunity to interview him. As we talked, there was a dog perched on Scholl's right shoulder named "Aileron."

Scholl was in Yuma to perform for the community's Military Appreciation Days. The irony of his comments still strikes me. Scholl explained to us about the risk of stunt flying looking worse than it is. "I'm a bleeder, and I'll bleed and I'm a coward too. So you know, I'm very careful. It may look like some real spectacular, fantastic things," noting it might appear you're cheating death every time you fly but it's not that way. "I do airplane crashes for the movies. I do a lot of stunts that are very, very hair-raising but the stunts are very well calculated. However, on the other hand you gotta' say that there aren't too many stunt pilots around. They're all dead." Scholl was referring to an article he read in "Flying" magazine that was talking about him. "They said (Scholl's) the highest paid guy in

Hollywood but he's the only one left alive." That got him thinking. and he said in our 1984 interview "I've been doing this for quite a few years and I did look back and yes, all our other stunt pilots have been killed. So we have to be very careful and calculate everything we do."

The day before he talked with us, Scholl had been flying for "Blue Thunder." He explained stunt pilots fly all kinds of airplanes including ones they've never flown. He made the point that normally, "if you're gonna' fly a military airplane you take a half a year's training. There's ground school and all that and here in this business we jump from one airplane into another and there are planes we've never flown before." Scholl once counted and discovered he had flown 186 types of airplanes. "I didn't know there were that many types until I started looking up and counting and choreographing what we've been flying. It can be a dangerous business if you let things go wrong."

When we talked, Scholl was chairman of the Aircraft Safety Committee and it had set up new rules for stunt pilots in the entertainment industry. "The stuntmen are out there highly paid to do a job and to take the risk away from the actors and to take the risk away from all the other surrounding people. If we go out and get killed that's part of our business but we're not to hurt anybody else in doing that." However, Scholl said stunt pilots try to protect themselves as well. "For instance, this Mohawk that I was flying. We went through the ground pyrotechnics to see that they had the proper stuff that wouldn't throw shrapnel and rocks up into the airplane as I made a machine gun pass." He added, "when the ground explosions came they had rocks on top of it and the rocks hit the airplane. We took about 37 hits, broke the windshield and actually the rocks went into the turbine engines and destroyed the engines, so we had some real problems." They had gone through the procedure before the flight, but what the pyrotechnic crew showed them on the ground was not what the crew did once the plane was in the air. Said Scholl, "they thought 'ah well, we're being overcautious.' Well we're not."

The safety rules included keeping innocent people far from the area. Actors and others are kept away from the stunt so if there's a crash they aren't hit with flying parts. Sometimes actors have to be in the immediate area but Scholl said they advise them of the risk and give them the option of moving back to the 500-foot line. Scholl believed it wasn't fair to not tell someone of the risk. "Suddenly they're exposed to something that in no wild idea that they would imagine a helicopter is gonna' fall out of the sky or a fixed wing is gonna' take their head off. But you tell 'em beforehand and then if they're in there and there's an accident, well that's part of the business."

Less than two years before we talked, actor Vic Morrow, perhaps best known for his role in the TV series "Combat," was filming a segment of the movie, "The Twilight Zone." Scholl said the warning wasn't given on on the set on July 23, 1982, in Indian Dunes, California. The scene called for Morrow to be running with two children with a helicopter flying overhead. The aircraft crashed, killing Morrow and the children.

Scholl saw the value of only hiring professionals. At the time he said, "the accidents that have happened have been non-stuntmen and non-movie pilots and people that are trying desperately to get into the business and when they do, they'll do anything for you. You ask them, they'll do it. But you ask a stuntman or a professional pilot and we'll say 'well, now wait a minute now, can't we use a longer lens on the camera and how about doing it this way, because we can't jeopardize this house or these people' and we change it. But we know how to say no, and the newcomers don't."

When Scholl was killed in 1985, the industry lost a talented performer and a strong advocate for safety and common sense in the entertainment business.

IN RADIO THE LIGHTING AND MAKEUP ARE ALWAYS PERFECT

WHEN THE CHANCE came to guest host a local television show I took it. I filled in several times for Gracie Hammons, a popular local talk show host in Yuma. I was in radio for a long time in Yuma, but all you have to do is host a TV show and you immediately get recognized at an intersection. That seldom happens in radio unless you say, "hey, I'm on the radio. Recognize me?"

I was used to doing interviews in a small radio studio or even at remote broadcasts but this was quite different, at least at first. The "living room" TV set was in a corner of a cavernous television studio that was similar to a small aircraft hangar. This may sound "new age" but when you're talking to people sitting across from you in a large TV studio, even if they're sitting close, the "energy" of the interview is diffused. It's as if you were talking to someone sitting on your couch, in the middle of a football field. I'm just saying it's harder to focus and generate the interview's required energy. It's almost as if I had to keep the energy level up in the whole building instead of just between the interviewee and me. But I loved doing the TV shows.

A TV host is there for you to see face to face. Well okay, just face, since they can't see you in person, at least with today's technology. But radio's "theatre of the mind" can create some unusual impressions. A good example of that is my buddy Mike Fender. He was the live DJ on Yuma's KVOY AM. Mike was a great example of a DJ who didn't look the way he sounded. With his long straight hair and a beer in one hand, Mike was a throwback to the hippie days. I guess Mike comes as close as anyone I've worked with to matching the demeanor of Dr. Johnny Fever on television's "WKRP in Cincinnati," except that Mike is not a burned out hippie and is a much more decent and upright guy than I imagine Fever would have been, were he real. Fever, I mean, not Fender. Mike was entertaining, funny and low key; favorite DJ traits for me. The fact that he's a biker who looks like Willie Nelson would probably never have occurred to his listeners. But that's the thing about radio. Not everyone looks the way they sound. People told me they thought I was a large person and younger. I know I'm not younger, but personally, I think 5'4" is large, at least compared to Meinhardt Raabe of Munchkinland. You'll meet him elsewhere in the book.

Sure, television or movies can present phony images but real ones too. It's an interesting experience to interview someone and later see them portrayed in a movie, as I did with Tom Sullivan. I talked with him at Arizona Western College when he came for an appearance.

WHEN I SAW **THE MOVIE** "If You Could See What I Hear" portraying Sullivan's life as an actor, father and blind person, I got the same sense of Sullivan from the actor in the movie that I had witnessed in the real person. How often in other professions do you get to see film biographies and watch the actor and then get to compare it with your firsthand knowledge of the real person? Purty nifty, huh, this interviewing gig?

Sullivan pointed out that he thought life is "a celebration of human uniqueness." But he said "we are all programmed to think negatively" and we all have what he called an "inconvenience." In his case it was his blindness but he said for others it can include shyness, or the feeling you're too heavy, the fear of growing old, or other issues. He said the way you deal with your disability can determine your success or failure in life. Sullivan wanted people to think of him as a father, husband, singer, a songwriter, a talk show host, an athlete and "maybe then down the line, seventh or eighth or ninth, a blind person." He said if we can "move the label system deeper into the way in which we're known, we have the chance to really revamp society."

He believed a disability does not make you who you are and that every disadvantage can be turned into a positive advantage. Sullivan wasn't saying his blindness had been easy, but he said it was a benefit. He said "in my whole life I've never met an ugly person, unless they chose to be."

I KEEP LOOKING FOR BIG CITY RADIO. OKAY, HOW ABOUT MEDIUM CITY?

IN MY QUEST for the big city I left Yuma for a job in a medium market in Stockton. This job in California probably should have taught me a lesson right then. The jobs you really want can turn into a disaster. That was the case in Stockton, at the University of the Pacific radio station, KUOP. It was a terrible fit for me. It did however, give me a great chance to once again cover a Ronald Reagan appearance. It was a 1984 presidential reelection campaign speech Reagan gave on the steps of the State Capitol in Sacramento. As president it must have felt triumphant for him to return to the statehouse where he had served as California governor.

Ronald and Nancy Reagan along with Frank Sinatra in 1984 as Reagan campaigns at the California Capitol for another term as President

The speaker's stand, covered in red, white and blue bunting and banners, included Ronald Reagan, along with his wife Nancy, Frank Sinatra, and in what must have seemed odd to diehard Democrats, Rosie Grier. He's known as the very large ex-football player who was a supporter of Bobby Kennedy in 1968, and was even on the scene at the Ambassador Hotel in Los Angeles in 1968 to wrestle with Kennedy's assassin (or one of them, depending on whom you believe.) Now, Grier was here with all these Republicans.

As I look back on Reagan's speech I don't remember a lot of the content but if my memory is correct, more noticeable than the content was the tone. You really did come away feeling soothed by something in the flow or timbre of his voice. I know they called him the Great Communicator, but I usually thought that meant content, and then I would be surprised to watch him stammer and think to myself, "this is the great communicator?" But if the tone of your voice can lull a person into feeling good, that is one great communicator and that was Reagan.

My time in Stockton also brought me up close and personal with civil rights activist, socialist and former member of the Black Panther movement Stokely Carmichael, who by then called himself Kwame Toure

I was in Stockton less than a year when I moved to Sacramento to work for KFBK as a morning news editor. I didn't get much chance to prove myself there and I was gone from that station in a month. I was certainly not on a winning streak. About the only thing I remember is a lot of needless pressure and I also recall one of the station's local talk show hosts named Rush Limbaugh, who would one day go to New York and develop a pretty good following.

He left KFBK after I did, though my departure and his weren't connected. Hmm, at least I don't think so. Maybe I should look into that. I do remember Rush sitting quietly at the station reading the paper. He also did local diet ads on television.

I only directly worked with him twice at KFBK that I recall. Once the computer was down during his local call-in show and I was holding up the name of the location of the caller for him. Another time I did a fill-in newscast with him working the control board, as we say in radio. I remember hitting a wrong button and him explaining why that was a wrong button. Apparently it sent out a recorded disclaimer of some sort. However, he seemed to be an okay guy considering his ego would soon become larger than the State Fairgrounds just down the street. It's surprising to think that Rush became so popular that people would stand in line just to meet him. I guess I should have paid more attention when I worked at KFBK.

That was, understandably, a low period for me -- not the first, not the last, but certainly a major one. I was fired from that Stockton radio station. Then I was fired from KFBK in Sacramento. I mean, losing two jobs in two months makes you think maybe everything is not coming up roses, no offense to singer Ethel Merman. You're supposed to lose jobs in radio. It's part of the business. But this can damage your ego a tad.

It took an employment agency to get me my next radio job. I had to decide. Should I stay in the Sacramento area and work peon jobs to pay the bills, or go back into radio by moving to Wyoming, a state that at the time I could barely find on the map? So I sat in a restaurant in Sausalito, California, with the beautiful bay and hills around me and tried to decide. That is not the best place to have an objective argument, even with yourself, as you know if you've been to the San Francisco Bay area. San Francisco? Wyoming? San Francisco? Wyoming? In a last minute decision I figured I'd head out to Wyoming and of course in radio you have an open file with moving companies. So I loaded up the rented trailer and hit the highway.

Wyoming was totally unexpected, and in some ways, a wonderful surprise! Now, I've always said how much I like greenery. It's part of what I loved in Northern California and also what I liked when I later moved to the Chicago area. But I grew up in the desert of Arizona, so I know and appreciate barren, and Wyoming has barren and then some. However, even being from expansive Arizona I was impressed with the wide-open spaces in Wyoming. This isolation, though, meant if I wanted to have a talk show with some out-of-town celebrities, I often, but not always, had to reach out with the telephone. That was the case for my talk with "debunker" James Randi. I was on the high plains of Wyoming at KRKK AM and KQSW FM. He was in a Los Angeles motel room.

JAMES "THE AMAZING" RANDI

"A postman from San Francisco has now been healed of 11 different diseases by nine different faith healers in seven different cities in two genders. He has the healthiest ovaries of any postman in San Francisco."

If you believe in faith healing you won't appreciate this profile. If you think it's all a scam, you will find James "The Amazing" Randi a breath of fresh air. Randi was certainly not in the middle on this issue. The magician and scam "debunker" said in our 1987 interview he was angry politicians were not doing anything to stop what he said was a rampant practice, taking in billions of dollars a year "on this kind of nonsense," that he said claims to be a religious matter. Yet, in Randi's words it is "nothing more than a series of conjuring tricks and psychological trickery used to convince people A) that they are healed and B) that the preacher has, through divine intervention healed other people of normally unhealable diseases." Randi said the faith healers say they are able to heal "finances, broken marriages, lost homes, lost jobs, every kind of situation you can imagine, including of course, incurable diseases." Randi conducted a two-and-a-half year investigation into hundreds of cases of people who said they had been healed and ministers who claimed to have healed some of them. Randi said he found the claims to be "just so much nonsense."

Randi said faith healers give themselves an "out," if the "healing" isn't successful. He noted, "they're always very careful to let God stay holding the bag when something goes wrong, and/or the victim, because they always say very clearly, 'I don't heal you. God heals you. And if God chooses not to bring His divine healing to you, well, then, there's something wrong in the way you're running your life.' So that is the guilt that is laid upon the victim."

He added "they strike the person on the forehead or they give them the oil or whatever they're going to do in order to heal them." Or, Randi said they look at them over the TV set "and point at them and say, 'you're now healed, thank you Jesus.'" But he said you're also reminded that if you don't keep that healing, "if it doesn't take, so to speak, if the seed doesn't sprout or whatever, then it's your fault because you didn't summon up enough faith." He pointed out that often, not summoning up enough faith is directly connected with not having made a large enough donation to prove your faith in God. I asked if the link with God lets the faith healer get away with not being medically licensed. He said they don't really make much of a claim that can be examined. Take Pat Robertson. Randi said, "(Robertson) will point out at a TV set and he will declare the woman out there with undiagnosed diabetes, for example. You didn't know you had diabetes but it is diabetes and it is now, through the grace of God, cured." Randi said there were hundreds of thousands of people watching this program at any one time in any location. He added, "probably many hundreds of little ladies out there who felt poorly yesterday or had a dizzy spell, or some such thing," thought Reverend Robertson was talking directly to them. So he said they go to their doctor who tells them they don't have a trace of diabetes and the patient says that's a healing. Randi said if they thought about it they would realize that the Robertson programs with the healings were often prepared weeks ahead, with a recording aired at different times in different parts of the country.

Randi worked with groups across the country to help him investigate claims of faith healing. Randi recalled a scam buster he sent to several "healings." He said, "a postman from San Francisco has now been healed of 11 different diseases by nine different faith healers in seven different cities in two genders. He actually went in drag on some of them. And...he has the healthiest ovaries of any postman in San Francisco."

When we talked in 1987, Randi said some faith healers had used what Randi referred to as the "calling out" gimmick. The preacher goes down the aisle and identifies someone and verifies the two have never spoken to each other. The minister then gives out personal information about the audience member. Randi pointed out, "what is not made evident is that he has sent someone down in the audience beforehand...to sit down and casually get into conservation with this person. All of this information has been extracted and it's either been transmitted by radio upstairs to the control room or it's been recorded one way or another and taken back to the preacher who then has this information at hand." Randi said it is made to look like divine knowledge directly from God. Randi has used fake names and diseases to prove what he said was the most important point. "If this man really is talking to God, then God would say 'no, that man is James Randi. That is not --' whoever the name is that I had worked up at that moment."

A dramatic Randi exposure of fakery involved Peter Popoff. Randi recalled, "we found out that Popoff not only was using the 'gift of knowledge' gimmick by sending his wife down along with other people in his hire to get into casual conversations" but Randi said Popoff's people were transmitting it upstairs to a control room, and Popoff "was making notes and watching on the TV monitors who they were speaking to. And then later on, when he went out onto the floor to get the divine inspiration from God, his wife was transmitting to him on 39.170 megahertz and he had a secret receiver in his ear." Randi's group saw the receiver and "we figured that a man who is healing the deaf shouldn't be wearing a hearing aid." They used a sophisticated scanner to tap in on it. Randi's expose on the "divine" inspiration got national attention.

In our 1987 interview Randi pointed to Popoff's literature that encouraged you to take that savings for a car or vacation and lend it to Jesus, "which means to send it to him, of course."

Despite the view that "God loveth a cheerful giver," Randi said givers are not all that cheerful and that some have been driven into bankruptcy by the pleas from the faith healers. He pointed to a famous incident when Oral Roberts told his followers that he would die if they didn't come up with eight million dollars. Yet, Randi said, Roberts could have sold his racehorses, cattle or mansions. "These people are extracting huge amounts of money by literally threatening their followers with hell and damnation if they don't come up with it." Roberts lived for a number of years after that, dying in 2009.

Some Christians accused Randi of being the anti-Christ or the Devil or something along that line. He said that attitude has been encouraged by preachers "who also tell them in so many words that they must not think, because thinking is a tool of Satan and thinking leads to questions, questions lead to doubt and doubt leads to loss of salvation."

When we talked James Randi had been at his work for 35 years and he couldn't prove there wasn't any authentic faith healing, at least until he said he had examined every case and he said there were hundreds of millions of claims down through the ages and it's not possible to prove that. Randi said he was "very much like the man who had been sitting for 35 years on December the 24th by his chimney, waiting patiently all night to see if a man in a red suit bounces down the chimney with a bag of toys." But he was quite definite when he said, "every opportunity that I've had to examine this claim has shown that it does not hold water."

HERE'S A SPORT YOU CAN PLUNGE INTO HEAD FIRST

WYOMING, AS YOU may guess, is a state of outdoor lovers. I guess I should say lovers of outdoors, otherwise it implies another possible outdoor sport. That love of the outdoors certainly existed in the Skinner family, a family of mountain climbers. Courtney Skinner launched a Wyoming Centennial Expedition to Mount Everest.

When we talked he passed along an interesting spin on the old line from famous Mount Everest climber Edmund Hillary. When asked why he climbed Everest, Hillary's famous line was "because it's there." Today, we tend to think it has some deep philosophical meaning, or at least I did. Even in the 1960s President John Kennedy quoted the line in his lofty pitch to send Americans to the moon. But Skinner told me that famous line wasn't so meaningful. He said it was meant, believe it or not, as a flippant remark. History is quirky sometimes.

Courtney's son Todd Skinner of Pinedale, Wyoming and Todd's partner Paul Piana were the first to free climb the "Salathe" Wall at Yosemite's El Capitan. In 1988, he and his fellow Wyoming climber traveled to the "head wall" in Yosemite and they almost didn't survive it. Said Todd, "the wall is 3600 feet. We slept on it for 37 nights, just on ledges or on hanging cots...Water becomes the most precious thing up there because you're working in the sun and you're working all day, yet water weighs seven pounds a gallon." He said they left the ground with 270 pounds of food, water and equipment so "the work load was terrible."

Todd Skinner 1958-2006

An accident at the end of the climb almost ruined the trip and almost took their lives, but probably the priority would be reversed. They made it to the top and both were on the summit. Skinner said, "right as we pulled our bags over the summit...the rock that we were attached to...using as an anchor, (fell) off the lip. (The rock) was something we'd used twice that year already and people always used." Skinner said it was about the size of a van, weighing many tons. The block cut loose and Skinner got caught between the rock sliding over the edge and a rope that was around his back. There was a constriction for about a full slow second that broke his ribs and did some other damage. The rope behind him broke and he went off the edge. It was a drop of more than 3000 feet they had just climbed. Fortunately, Skinner was saved by a device attached to the ropes. The rock ground over his partner's leg, breaking four bones. The rope carrying about 100 pounds of gear was cleanly cut, sending it 3600 feet to the trees below. In fact, all of the ropes were cut, except one.

If you're a climber, you know what he was talking about when he described an ascender, clamped to the rope. It allows one man to climb while another follows up the rope, leaving his hands free. The ascender was crushed at the level where the other ropes were cut, but this rope hung on. Six inches placement of the ascender in either direction and his rope would have been cut, sending Skinner falling thousands of feet.

Skinner said his partner thought Skinner had fallen and was gone, but then he saw the smashed ascender and saw Skinner's bloody hand grab it. The rock cut the ropes so cleanly they appeared to have melted. Said Skinner, "when (extreme pressure) pinches something, it burns it (and the ropes were) all just melted at those areas and the ascender was ruined." My guess is that an ascender was a small price to pay to avoid a 3600 foot fall.

The experience didn't make Todd Skinner leery of climbing. "The odds were unbelievable against it happening and then we realized at the same time that since it did happen the odds were unbelievable that we didn't go with our haul bags to the ground...We were extremely fortunate. If I could climb right now I would." But, at the time, Skinner was recovering from his injuries to his bones and muscles.

Listening years later to my interview of Todd Skinner tell the story again after all these years, I think I'm even more astounded at what a dramatic story this is. As a transplanted desert dweller in a cold Wyoming climate I figured I was lucky just walking on ice in winter and not falling. But this redefines lucky!

After a career of climbing around the world, Skinner, who was just shy of his 48th birthday, was back in Yosemite in October 2006 rappelling down the so-called "Leaning Tower." There was a harness failure and Skinner fell 500 feet to his death. He had many achievements over the years but his website describes his climb up the Salathe Wall in 1988 as ushering in "a new dawn of climbing."

I'VE HEARD OF BASKING IN THE GLOW, BUT...

VLADIMIR NESTERENKO WAS probably lucky too, considering where he had been. This day, though, the Russian was in Rock Springs, Wyoming; an obvious transition, right? Actually when I met him, Vladimir was a Soviet citizen in the U.S., as he put it, "under the protection of the United States Government."

He once was an engineer working with the Soviet Department of Energy. Three days after the 1986 Chernobyl nuclear plant disaster, he was sent to the site to help rebuild and safeguard the reactor.

In his soft, yet pronounced Russian accent, he told me he was quite surprised by the scope of the catastrophe and what was left after the explosion. In his slightly rough, yet still very good English, he told me, "first of all, I was impressed by the extent of the damaging of the reactor itself," he said. "It was the strange coincidence of several mistakes, made by the maintenance workers, operators and engineers." Nesterenko said the government test was not properly prepared. He said the accident couldn't be blamed on the reactor design. The alarm monitoring system was disconnected and he said the main cause was an increase in the water flow and a decrease in the steam power inside the reactor, affecting the efficiency of the reactor and leading to the explosion.

Nesterenko said at the time of our interview other countries needed to learn to work together on problems and in 1986 he was urging the opening of the then-Soviet Union so information could get out. When we talked, he told me he had radiation sickness. "I will suffer it for some time," he told me, "but I was taking medical treatment and that's why I feel myself better."

Speaking of nuclear power, I did get to tour a nuke plant under construction. That was back when I was working in Yuma. We flew to the site west of Phoenix, called Palo Verde, owned by the utility company called Arizona Public Service. As they took us through the construction area they were quite open about the system and procedure, but of course with a positive spin on nuclear power. What worries a lot of people and deservedly so, is what to do with nuclear waste. That waste will be around almost as long as it takes me to sell all of the copies of my book. In other words, thousands of years. A half-life is nothing compared to a shelf life.

The shelf life of a musician is sometimes limited too. So maybe it helps to have four musicians in a group because this group proved it had staying power.

RANDY OWEN, TEDDY GENTRY, JEFF COOK, MARK HERNDON

"If we took the fiddle out of stuff we do, we'd probably have been on the pop charts in the '60s."

The country western group that became known as "Alabama" began playing in the early 1970s, but it wasn't until 1980 that the song, "Tennessee River" from the movie, "Urban Cowboy" brought them to the national scene. In the 1980s, "Alabama" had taken the Country Music Association Top Vocal Group of the Year award, the Entertainer of the Year award from the Academy of Country Music, and the Academy of Country Music Artist of the Decade honor. The awards would continue for years. When I talked to the group it included members and cousins lead singer Randy Owen, Teddy Gentry and Jeff Cook. Drummer Mark Herndon joined the group in the early days of playing in South Carolina, though he later left. The four came to where I was working, the high country of Rock Springs, not to sing, but to sign autographs. It was 1988 and the band was riding high. But when they talked to us reporters they were riding a bus, from the Rock Springs airport to a local shopping mall. Singer Randy Owen told me they had just finished playing at the Forum in Los Angeles. Now, here they were on the high plains of Wyoming with few people and wide-open spaces. But Owen told me he wasn't a city person. "This is a whole different world. This is the world I prefer over L.A."

The grind of being on the road didn't stop the group from being out there, so to speak. In fact, just the opposite. Said Owen, "you know, we dreamed of success for years and years. Whatever you do, there's sacrifice involved in it. It'd be easier on everybody just to stay home, I guess, but there's a motivation a way down deep that, you know, you dream of playing music for a living, you dream of all the things that can happen, and luckily for us, and thank God it happened, and we got a chance to, you know, be successful in music." He added, "I dreamed of days being able to come to places like this -- how the fans appreciate your being there so much." It didn't take much for Owen to get up for a show. "I have to see just a few of the kids' eyes and see 'em light up when we get off of the plane or see them when we first see 'em and you know, I'm ready to go."

When we talked in '88, Owen said it was important for the fans to know the group and the individuals in it. He had a number of opportunities to go out as a single act but at that time said, "that's not something I want to do, so I haven't done it. I enjoy what I do now. There's not time to do all these careers and everything." The idea of double the travel didn't seem feasible. He laughed when he said, "I couldn't do it."

Guitarist Jeff Cook agreed getting out on the road was part of the job. He felt if you're going to continue making records (now music streaming and Internet radio, of course) you can make all the recordings in the world but if you don't get out and tour and support the recordings then you're spinning your wheels.

He told me their concerts sometimes drew both country and rock fans. "Our encore consists of things like "Taking Care of Business," "Heard It Through the Grapevine," "Hello, I Love You," "Satisfaction." In 1988 Cook didn't know where country music would be in ten years. He laughed when he said, "I don't know, but I hope we're still playing it." It was his theory that "country was about 20 years behind rock." Cook remembers when he was 14 and starting in radio in 1964. The music being played was Paul Revere and others. "If we took the fiddle out of the stuff we do, we'd probably have been on the pop charts in the '60s." Was that okay with him? Cook said it suited him. "I'm not really an old line, hard core country person, either. There are some legends in there like George Jones and Merle Haggard, which we got to work with last night and I still sometimes can't comprehend that 'cause to me they are the stars, we're still the new kid on the block." Maybe that "new kid" view has changed in the years since our interview.

Cook found some relaxation by playing in clubs. After a concert he would go and hear a band and sit in with them. It gave him a chance to play something other than the regular songs. He said some of the other guys didn't want to go back to the clubs, but Cook owned part of a club and he played there, as well as sitting in with bar bands on the road. "It's like a plumber going home and workin' on his own pipes. It promotes good will too, I think."

"Alabama" member Teddy Gentry told reporters on this Wyoming bus that there were many nights playing in Myrtle Beach, South Carolina, and in clubs in the Southeast. "I don't think any of us could have visualized how far "Alabama" would go, but, you know, the success is not "Alabama." The success is measured in units, people that like what we do." Gentry felt fortunate to have "put out something that people wanted to hear and that they're willing to pay for," and he said, "we work hard at what we do. We've got the best crew in the world, I think, and try to take care of the fans, but they definitely take care of us." Comparing country fans to rock fans, Gentry said he thought the hard core country fans who really like you are more likely to "hang with you" for a longer period. "Over the years, you know, they still like you." Gentry said a lot of young people came to their shows. "I like to feel like we've turned a lot of young people on to country music, maybe." Gentry said whether you're laying brick, being a cowboy or whatever, success takes hard work. He noted a lot of entertainers don't want the life on the road, but "Alabama" was willing to do everything it could and take advantage of every situation to promote its music.

Drummer Mark Herndon said "Alabama" made itself more accessible to fans and media than probably anyone else who was on the road at that time. The excited crowds never ceased to amaze him. "You get so used to doing this for a living and you kinda' think, 'what are they all so excited about?' cause, you know, you don't consider yourself anybody special. I put, you know, both legs in a pair of jeans just like everybody else. So I don't see it from their perspective. It's pretty wild."

Herndon joked with the Wyoming reporters on this bus that the band had not considered changing its name from "Alabama" to "Wyoming." As Herndon put it, "Alabama" obviously starts with an "A" and he said that was first in the record rack. So for obvious reasons "Wyoming" wouldn't be their choice of names. Of course, these days it's maybe an alphabetical listing on a website, but the logic probably holds true.

WHEN YOU'RE SIX FOOT, SEVEN, IT'S EASY TO HAVE FRIENDS IN HIGH PLACES

ONE OF WYOMING'S now former senators made a small name for himself, partly as the co-author of a bill on immigration, partly as a good buddy of the first President Bush and partly as an outspoken critic of Democrats and the press. All of those parts add up to a guy who's six foot seven. It wasn't an easy interview physically for me my height of five foot four, but sometimes we were seated and that put me more eye to eye with Senator Alan Simpson -- well, closer to his eye, anyway.

We got into a dispute once over something that popped up again with the Republican "Contract with America" in the '90s. It's the idea that Congress should follow the same rules the rest of America follows. That's still an issue. I applied to be a field representative to run the constituents office in Rock Springs. During the job interview with his staff, I was asked my family status and political views. That upset me, particularly because I had read an article where Senator Simpson criticized Congress for not following the hiring guidelines private industry had to follow. Well, that's why the questions from the staff seemed all the more inappropriate. So I wrote the senator a letter saying I was offended and pointed out to him that the questions might even be illegal if they had been asked at an interview in the private sector. The next time I saw him he told me it was a good letter. Okay fine, it was a good letter, but I wondered what he would do about it? He then sent me a letter saying how important his office staff people were and "there was never any intention of my staff to make any kind of invasion upon your privacy." Instead, he said what "makes you tick...very closely relates to your employment in our staff operation." That didn't fully answer my concerns, but wasn't it a nice letter?

Covering school and teacher related issues seemed to come naturally to me. I don't know why, except I can appreciate the fervor of the profession. Teachers do seem to have an underlying passion for their craft, but really get heated up over their salaries. I've worked for low radio salaries, so it's like the old saying, "been down so long it looks like up to me." However, in a perfect world, everyone, teachers and broadcasters, would get what they're worth.

Evidently my education coverage was thorough because I did win the Sweetwater County Education Association Award and the next step, the statewide Wyoming Education Association Award. When I went to accept the WEA statewide award, I think I hit the right tone when I addressed the group in Casper, Wyoming. I told them news doesn't operate in a vacuum and reporters need the cooperation of their sources. Unwittingly, I think I boosted the WEA officer election campaign for the head of the Sweetwater group with those comments about how he had worked with me. But that's okay. I didn't try to cater to the teachers. I was objective. They liked what I did, but, no, I wasn't in their back pocket.

Ethics questions are a constant in newswriting. At least they should be. You have to have a good sense of what you believe when you are called upon to make daily decisions. For example, I had one candidate talking about a bridge replacement important to the area. He surely knew where the bridge would be built, but in the interview sound bite he referred to the wrong river. I had a couple of choices when I wrote that story. I could use the cut with the error and make him appear ignorant or I could understand he just made a mistake and that the error didn't show a lack of knowledge of the issues. I chose to use another sound cut. If the campaign were about his geographic illiteracy, then the cut with the error would have been relevant. Or if grammar were the issue and he sounded functionally illiterate, that would have played a part in my decision. Otherwise, you take the high road, as I think most of my sister and brother broadcasters would do. At least I hope so.

Our radio station in Rock Springs was an AM-FM combination. Rock Springs is a remote area, although right along Interstate 80. The station itself was a bit out of the main part of town.

That's the station on the left and the area with my apartment building on the right. Not that far a walk really, but neither were in the center of town.

Rock Springs and its closest neighbor, Green River, are about 180 miles east of Salt Lake City, and both towns are north of the popular fishing area called Flaming Gorge along Interstate 80. Anyway, sometimes I felt quite isolated from the real world. In other ways the world seemed quite real there as you watched wild horses along the road or met people who really liked where they were and were quite involved in the daily routine in this small community. At the time there were roughly 30,000 people, combining Green River and Rock Springs.

Sweetwater County alone, where I lived (also alone), is about the size of Maryland, in square miles, although the entire state of Wyoming had less than 500,000 people when I was there. A Wyoming official described the state as one small town with very long streets. I'm not a fan of small towns, even though sometimes I really miss Wyoming, except when I think about wanting to go shopping or to a full size airport, but Salt Lake City was a long way to go.

There is an upside. A small town radio station has a small staff and when you're the news director/trash controller/bottle washer, you get to meet a lot of great people and do some nifty things. Among them was the time I helped raise a cement statue when a local professor tried to determine how the famous heads on Easter Island might have been moved. My theory is UPS shipped them, but the facts don't support that. One problem the original builders of the Easter Island statues of heads didn't face (pun intended) was the incredible cold weather we had that day in Rock Springs.

A bunch of us grabbed a rope and tried to move the re-created statue. Then we tried pulling it along some log rollers and then added the power of a pickup truck. I don't believe this was the authentic way of moving it, because, as I understand ancient history, pickup trucks didn't come along until the early 1700s. (Which doesn't explain the camper shells found all over the island.) Our cement statue fell over and cracked. We stopped there. The original occupants of Easter Island of course, huddled into their medium size luxury cars and got away before anyone could ask them about the task.

There were some national political bigwigs who were Wyoming residents. My congressman was Dick Cheney, who, before he was secretary of Defense, before he was vice president, was on my talk show. Be careful you're not hurt by the names I'm dropping.

You may hear your member of Congress complain about the size of his or her district. Consider instead what Dick Cheney and others running for Congress have faced. In Wyoming, Wyoming is the district. The whole state, of course, has two senators but just one member of Congress. With such a sparse population, as someone aptly put it, you have to go 200 miles for 200 votes. Then-Congressman Cheney was the same way he appeared when he reemerged on the national interview scene as Vice President Cheney, easygoing and intelligent. However, from a reporter's perspective I didn't find him to be the easiest interview. That's a selfish view, but I say that because he didn't confine his answers to 20-second sound bites. The ability to give short answers is important, though, for local and national media exposure. Although I admit, Cheney did well without that talent.

From what he once told me I can only guess that a national election night fascinated him. Cheney told me he enjoyed crunching election statistics and he had many post election weeks to do that, when he wasn't helping put together a new administration as he did years later for then President-elect George W. Bush.

Dick Cheney was also President Gerald Ford's chief of staff in the 1970s. He told me it kept him quite busy. I don't know if that contributed to his heart troubles, but he seemed pretty mellow when I knew him. I got the impression from what I was told that his mellow nature was a change from his earlier self. Of course you never know when someone is churning on the inside. I think I'm churning now. Butter him than me. Get it? Butter? Churning? I'll move on.

'TIS THE SEASON FOR BIG TALKING

IN THE PRESIDENTIAL primary season of 1988, several candidates came a'callin' to Rock Springs, among them Al Gore, one of a pack of Democrats running for the White House that year. We reporters gathered in a banquet room at a local motel where Gore would attend a political reception in his honor. We were seated at a long table, perpendicular to the lectern. Gore arrived and apologized for being late. He had overslept and then had gone jogging. Before the press conference began he went down the reporters' table introducing himself to each of us, a rather gracious gesture I think.

If elected in 1988, Gore, at age 40, would have been the youngest president in American history. I asked him if age were a factor in the campaign. He said, in his soft Tennessee drawl, "it has been an advantage more than a disadvantage." He pointed out there would only be two years difference between his age and that of John Kennedy's when he was elected or Theodore Roosevelt when he became president. Gore said, "the more debates and televised joint appearances there are, the less that becomes a factor of any kind. When people have a chance to see all the candidates together on the same stage they realize that what's far more important than numerical age is experience." Gore said his resume in that election season included 12 years in the House and Senate and he said that was more experience than the majority of candidates in the presidential race. He added there was one other factor. "There is a pendulum effect in presidential elections, with people searching out what people don't have at the time." He said in the election of 1960 the nation went from the oldest president to serve as of that time (Eisenhower) to the youngest president ever elected as of that time (Kennedy). "By coincidence, in 1988 we have a chance to do exactly that again," he said, meaning a transition from incumbent Ronald Reagan to Al Gore. It didn't happen that year but you have to wonder how much he kept thinking about that pendulum effect.

Wyoming reporters talked with Illinois U.S. Senator Paul Simon as he came "to call" in 1987, running for president, and it would be five years after that Wyoming visit before I would interview him again, after I had moved to Illinois. Funny how that works. He looked at me strangely when I told him how much I liked the song, "Sound of Silence." Well, I didn't really say that to the senator. Not that he probably hadn't heard that joke one or two thousand times. The two Paul Simons, senator and singer, even appeared together on the TV show "Saturday Night Live," once, playing off that confusion.

Senator and author Paul Simon died in 2003 at the age of 75.

Years after we met on the plains of Wyoming I again interviewed Senator Simon in Wilmington, Illinois

When a famous gymnast came to town (no phone interview here) the tie-in with politics should have been obvious. Both are flexible, resilient and cute as a button. Well okay, that doesn't apply to politics, but it did to Cathy Rigby.

CATHY RIGBY

"I don't know what the magic is exactly, except that they're so tiny and they do these incredible feats."

Cathy Rigby never thought she paid too high a price for her gymnastics. When I talked with her in the late 1980s, the onetime Olympian told me she never looked on it as giving up other things. "I didn't really care that I missed too much of the social activities because there was no place I'd rather be than in the gym." But there was a price to pay. Rigby said the way she grew up she didn't learn a lot about responsibility and life in general, and how to deal with people, and how to communicate, because she was sheltered most of the time by a coach. "Basically, my personality was determined by how I performed and that was my life," she said. The only things she really missed were a lot of life issues that affected her later. She said that's pretty typical of young athletes, noting, "I think we are more aware of it, you know, as coaches, that we need to develop and make these kids more well-rounded." She pointed out kids must learn that dedication is okay and motivation is good. "but you have to also teach during that time an awful lot about responsibility and putting things in perspective, and winning and losing." Rigby said it isn't as obvious as we think it is. "I think you really, as a coach and as a parent, have to teach that to your kids."

Rigby very badly needed to prove herself through sports, and because body weight was such an issue, and perfection and control were so important, she developed an eating disorder. "I was anorexic and bulimic for 12 years throughout my gymnastic career, as well as after I retired from the sport. I think had I little bit more on the ball as far as my personal life was concerned, and had my coach and possibly my parents been a little more aware of developing that side, I don't think I would have gotten into that problem."

It took nine years after her gymnastics career ended for her to realize her life was not going in the right direction. "Basically I went through a lot of personal problems, including divorce and things like that. But the one thing these problems taught me is that I could take control of my own life and I could learn responsibility." At the time, she had two children and had to learn responsibility and she says if she weren't the one to do it, no one else would. She also got a lot of support from a man she married in 1982, who showed her how her sports background had opened doors to her and that was something she shouldn't throw away.

It may seem ironic to look at people who have so much going for them, and see them face such insecurity. However, Rigby pointed to top athletes and movie stars, who, in her view, many times "get to where they are because they've had this incredible desire to prove something for some insecurity that they had early in their life or whatever, and if they don't work it out somewhere along the line, then they tend to be destructive with their life." As examples, she listed people like singer Karen Carpenter and comedic actor John Belushi. Rigby said we have to put our lives in perspective before we start hero worshipping, because many people on the pedestal are as insecure as we are and need to get their lives together.

Rigby's first Olympics were in 1968 in Mexico. You might remember or have read of the "black power" salute given by two of the athletes. At her Olympic competition in 1972, Arab terrorists killed some Israeli athletes. So political issues have appeared at the games, but she said, "there's no greater feeling than walking out on that field with all these great athletes who have...like many athletes, dedicated their life to doing something good." In 1987's interview, Rigby didn't believe politics would tear the

Olympics down. "I think the athletes are too strong for that, and I think the…Olympic movement is too strong to let something like this happen." At the time of our interview Rigby said, "they've gone through so much turmoil over the years, and yet they've still managed to keep their head above water and keep going."

Even after the terrorism at the Olympics in Munich in 1972, she says the athletes went on because they didn't want the terrorism to pull them down. "I think, out of that terrible tragedy, came athletes pulling together in brotherhood and love for each other, cutting across any political beliefs to just coming together as a whole for those athletes who died. They have a lot of respect for each other that goes beyond all the politics, and I think that's why the whole world looks on, because it is so positive."

Have you wondered why gymnasts capture America's attention? In our interview Rigby found it funny that every four years, "for some reason, there is a gymnast that comes out on the cover of Wheaties or whatever." Rigby, who stood just under five feet tall, added, "we never looked like we were old enough to even be there," noting, "they're the smallest of athletes, obviously. I don't know what the magic is, exactly, except that they're so tiny and they do these incredible feats, especially nowadays, and I think they just capture everybody's heart. They're just loveable… like…little teddy bears." She noted a lot of parents look at their own daughters who stand on their heads wanting to be little gymnasts. "How can you not love children? And that's what they look like out there, little children," said Rigby, laughing.

Rigby didn't get into gymnastics until age ten and believe it or not, that was late in life. When we talked in '87 she said many of the athletes were then starting at age six or seven. "It's also because many of them have an awful lot more to learn than I did at that time." She did get a bit of a head start though, because she took ballet at age seven. At age ten, she didn't know about competition but got into gymnastics, "mainly because it was fun and I loved jumping on a trampoline and on the uneven bars and all of that, and then competition came later." She found it a little frightening "to have to prove myself every time I got up on the beam."

Despite her problems with the career, Rigby recommended gymnastics. It can be very dangerous, and as with any sport you have to pay attention to your child's coaching, but she felt if a child really loves gymnastics it's "perfectly great to get involved in" and "a wonderful sport." Rigby looked on the journey as more important than the final awards. "I think what I want young people in athletics or anything just to know that winning medals and being first and all of that isn't the most important thing. It's the process that is so important."

She believed you could gain so much from athletics or anything that you dedicate yourself to, but there's a caution. "You can't let somebody else determine your personality. You can't always be achieving for somebody else. You've gotta' do it for yourself, and because you love whatever you're doing and for the right reasons."

It was a hard road for her at times, but she came out the other side with some important knowledge. "I've learned a lot about success and failure, and I have learned that no matter what I do in life, if I put my mind to it and if I'm dedicated to that purpose…I can do anything I want, and I really believe that, and I think anybody else can." Rigby said at the time that every year in gymnastics an athlete will do a new trick and we think that's the best anyone can do. "We just put limits on ourselves," but she said, "we can't do that." She adds, "we can do anything we want."

Here I've told you how I had to often rely on the telephone to get some big name interviews but then I turn around and highlight some folks who actually came to the state. Cathy Rigby of course, in Rock Springs, and another was the onetime commander of U.S. forces in Vietnam. Though General William Westmoreland wasn't quite as accessible as Cathy Rigby. To talk to him I had to travel about 90 miles west to Evanston, Wyoming.

CAN A GENERAL HAVE A PRIVATE MOMENT?

JUST BECAUSE A CAREER is waning doesn't mean that person won't get a group of reporters, including people like me, to swarm around and pay a lot of attention. That was the case with former Vietnam Commander of U.S. forces and Army Chief of Staff General William Westmoreland. He came to Evanston all bedecked and bedazzling with ribbons and medals on his uniform. It was the dedication of a war memorial and that plays great in small towns.

He told me at the time,, "grassroots America has got more support for the veterans than metropolitan America. Why that is the case, I don't know, but it certainly is prevalent here today," the general said on that visit.

Movies were on his mind that day as he spoke against the just released movie, "Platoon." It's an anti military film and (big surprise) that didn't sit well with him. I asked him if there were a "Top Gun," "Rambo" mentality in the country. He said he thought younger Americans felt that service in uniform was honorable and necessary, and "if there is a bit of excitement and drama involved, I guess they don't object to that."

He hadn't seen a Rambo movie and said he never intended to, "but he said, "I don't think he wears a uniform. He's just some guy that goes berserk with a gun in his hand." He said you have to make the distinction between that and someone who legitimately serves his country in uniform. Maybe I should have asked him about the image of a former member of the Army's Special Forces and Vietnam vet hunted by police, which actually was the case with Rambo.

After our interview and then press conference Westmoreland was meeting and greeting folks in the plaza area. I had the original wirecopy where Henry Kissinger is quoted with his famous line that "peace is at hand" in Vietnam. I asked Westmoreland to sign it. He recognized me as one of the reporters and was reluctant to autograph the piece. I'm not sure why. He said I should get Kissinger to sign it. I said I hoped to and he relented and put his name to it. As a collector of history I think my persistence paid off because it may be a one of a kind document. Besides the historical content and then the signature, it is also a type of wirecopy you won't see anymore, now that digital wire services and higher tech printers have taken over. This was from the old phone line printers. They were noisy, big clunkers that would garble news copy when there was a phone line transmission problem. As I mentioned earlier, one of the machines used to sit behind my desk in my first radio job in Bisbee. Good riddance to those machines.

I DON'T CARE IF IT SLICES AND DICES, GET OFF MY LAWN

YOU MAY BE FAMILIAR with the Green River Ordinances. Towns around the country have enacted the law in one form or another but you may not know the original law started just west of Rock Springs in Green River, Wyoming. The idea was to keep door to door salespeople from knocking on your door. Local merchant T.S. Taliaferro wrote the law and it was adopted in 1931. Supposedly his motive was to protect the sleep of railroad workers at home. Since he was a local business owner, maybe he had other reasons to limit the competition, reasons known only to him and his store cash register.

Less than a year before his son Eddie Taliaferro died, I called the son at his home in Green River. He was 80 years old, but vividly recalled the days of the door to door sales. "Everybody was just selling door to door to door, (selling) everything. I mean strangers and local people too, were house to house selling."

His memory of his father was strong as well. He was, as Eddie put it, "a one in a million attorney."

In the son's view, the Green River Ordinance was a good law and he pointed out even Chicago almost put it in, but he says mostly encyclopedia salesmen fought that.

NOW FROM THE EXOTIC LAND WE CALL AMERICA

IT WAS A THRILL for me to become a global broadcaster and it wasn't even intentional. DXers, as they were called, (not to be confused with Gen Xers) in the Scandinavian countries would string radio reception wires through the trees above the Arctic Circle. They would record the radio signals they'd receive and write to the radio station for confirmation they had picked up that station's signal.

A small souvenir sent to our station from a listener on the other side of the globe

One tape we received at KRKK/KQSW in Rock Springs even came with a bonus -- Swedish music. One tape from a DXer actually had a little feature I had aired. There was a lot of static and if I didn't know the feature and the tone of my voice I wouldn't have known it was me. But it's pretty cool, don't you think, to know your voice has been heard among the reindeer? I'm not an engineer, but considering Wyoming is so far north, my guess is our signal bounced over the North Pole rather than taking any transatlantic route. Doesn't it make you wonder where else parts of you travel without your being aware? My voice went over the North Pole, but your picture could be in hundreds of family photo albums and you wouldn't know it. Remember that family at the Grand Canyon taking pictures and you're in the background, or those tourists at the Lincoln Memorial who were in front of you with a video camera? You may be traveling back home with them to distant lands, through the magic of video.

One time at KRKK/KQSW, I had a very pregnant goat in my office. The sad part is, I don't remember why. I know it was for an hour. Does that help? Oh, right, you don't know either why I had the goat.

I like to explore the areas where I'm living and Wyoming certainly lends itself to that. To be able to literally walk in the footsteps of the westward pioneers of the 1800s is a real charge. The Oregon Trail history is rich and very evident. This may surprise you, but in places, the wagon ruts on the trail are still there!

A fenced off section of Oregon Trail near where the famed Donner Party become the Donner Party and where you can literally "walk in the footsteps of the pioneers" Note the highway to the left that probably in 100 years may look as antiquated as this trail does to us.

As they passed through the many miles of open territory, the pioneer travelers would carve their names in rock. One time, an official of the Bureau of Land Management was driving reporters to one of those sites. The brittle shale rock was crumbling at the Immigrant Springs Wyoming Historic Site with Indian and western migration inscriptions in the rock and the BLM was trying to record the names before the carved history became a pile of pebbles. We drove out there on this dirt road that was actually part of the Oregon Trail. Now, I realize in Europe, the idea of using something 100 or more years old is no big deal, but in this country it is. Our BLM guide told us that driving on the trail was the BLM's form of low-level maintenance. Not a bad idea!

Along the Oregon Trail where pioneer inscriptions were being recorded before the shale crumbled and the inscriptions were lost to time.

Oregon Trail wagon ruts at Guernsey, Wyoming

It's interesting, too, that after 150 years or so pioneer graffiti becomes history. What does that say for the future of railroad underpasses? Is spray paint immortality assured?

Independence Rock about 50 miles southwest of Casper, Wyoming with pioneer immigrant inscriptions in the rock.

Since I'm in a history mode, (when we get to dessert I'll be in a pie "a la mode." Okay, sorry.) I'll tell you that during one vacation my camera and I headed north to Sheridan and across the Wyoming state line into Montana. I was heading for Custerland and I knew I was in the right area General George Custer traveled and excited when I saw the sign that said, "Little Big Horn River!"

Custer's Last Stand was on this lonely hill in south central Montana above the Little Big Horn River. The markers show where the soldiers fell. There are now also markers on the battlefield where Indians fell.

The Indian monument to the battle was placed at the top of the hill shortly before I visited, but the plan was to put it in the museum and install a better one.

As you come up on the site of the Battle of the Little Big Horn, you'll see the visitors' area to your right, along with a national cemetery that includes the grave of Major Reno, of General George Custer battle fame. To the left is a hill – Last Stand Hill. At the top of the hill is a large marker above the bodies of some of the 7th Cavalry. Stretching down the hill are not graves, but tombstone-like markers where the bodies of Custer's men were found. Custer's marker isn't any larger but it has a dark rather than white side to it.

The fight was known to Indians as the Battle of the Greasy Grass. You really feel history surrounds you. Down there, look, it's two or three markers where bodies where found. Over in that valley are two more markers and another over there. Since the land is still part of the Crow Indian reservation, at least when I was there you would see less modern-day intrusion than you might expect. There were no large billboards pitching arrowhead souvenirs, no signs to the Sitting Bull Bar and Wax Museum and certainly no Custerburgers. That's not to say there isn't somewhat of a tourist feel. I mean, you could drive your motorhome to the top of Last Stand Hill. But it could have been much worse. Not that I would want to see it restricted or isolated from the public, because that would mean less public understanding and appreciation. I say understanding, because when I was there it seemed to me that the historical presentation was trying to give a balanced view of the two sides.

Two weeks before I was there, Indians, under the guidance of leader Russell Means, had just put up their own marker at the top of the Last Stand Hill. It read, in part, "in honor of our Indian patriots who fought and defeated the U.S. Cavalry in order to save our women and children from mass murder. In doing so, preserving rights to our homelands, treaties and sovereignty."

Some of the commercialization I talked about showed up in a very small way. Most people wouldn't think twice about it, but on a receipt from the gift shop at 14:02 hours 7-9-88 it says, on the top:

CUSTER BATTLEFIELD
THANK YOU

Of course, always on the lookout (oops, bad choice of words, given the site), okay, always looking for that next great interview I was able to talk with one of the presenters at the battlefield. Lois was the great, great granddaughter of Curly, a scout for Custer. I asked her what Custer would think of the whole setting. There was the battlefield, the national cemetery and a small museum and gift shop. Lois said Custer wanted his name known and he got what he wanted. She said he wanted to be known "for generations to come. He made a name for himself."

I probably had not been there more than an hour and I already had heard two derogatory references to Custer. Lois said some visitors either really like him or totally dislike him. "I think the majority of them are sympathetic towards the Indian people who were here." She pointed out some were ashamed of what they may call a dark chapter in American history. In 1988 at least, Lois told me "the visitors today are objective. They want to know the whole story." She said one visitor was totally pro-Indian, but she felt that wasn't right either.

After taking it all in, absorbing the history, I left the Little Big Horn battlefield, which is more than George Custer was able to do.

A DISASTER? LET'S TALK

BEING A HISTORY buff really expands the topics I like to talk about on the air. One former NASA flight surgeon wrote a book about the space program and was out to promote it. (Boy, do I know what that's like!) Doctor Fred Kelly also headed the medical panel investigating the 1967 Apollo capsule fire that killed three American astronauts.

It was Kelly's view the astronaut corps, more than most people, feel something bad will happen to the other guy and not to them. On January 27, 1967 it happened to them. Astronauts Gus Grissom, Ed White and Roger Chaffee were inside their Apollo capsule during a ground test. A flash fire erupted, killing all three.

Fred Kelly was on duty that evening. He partially entered the charred cabin and called it one of the darkest times in his NASA career. "I have trouble even now talking about it," Kelly said at the time of our interview. "There was simply no chance of survival...We have pretty good evidence that Ed White tried very hard for at least 16 seconds to open the hatch and was unable to before he was overcome by the fumes." Kelly said it wasn't the fire but the carbon monoxide that killed them.

Investigators couldn't pinpoint the exact spark that caused the fire, but the atmosphere was pressurized with 100 percent oxygen. Kelly said, "almost anything will burn in an atmosphere like that. All you need is a spark and we knew that, but we'd gotten by with it before." But Kelly told me it was very difficult to stop a program in space to say, "hold on, this is not safe." Kelly added, "many things are not safe. It's not safe to fly in space and there are things that could stop almost any program at any point." He said the goal is to prevent all accidents but "we just aren't that smart, I'm afraid."

A short while after the phone interview, Dr. Kelly was driving his motorhome thrugh Wyoming and we were able to get together at a restaurant. It's always great to find interviewees who are genuinely nice people and Fred Kelly fell into that category.

YOU MEAN THERE ACTUALLY ARE PEOPLE LISTENING?

THE IMPACT OF radio can be surprising, even if you work in it. Once in Wyoming I did a drug show with some counselors. To promote the upcoming show, I used one of the counselors' voices talking about the strength of alcohol. One of her clients heard the promo, didn't know where the voice was coming from and was so shocked to hear it, the client decided not to go out and smoke pot, at least not that time. It's the power of the media, or maybe the power of a disembodied voice.

I know when I open the microphone that people are listening. I know this, intellectually. It's much tougher to know that emotionally. Years later I still was taken aback a bit (say that fast) when someone told me they listened. Not that I didn't love to hear that. Once I phoned a festival coordinating office and a woman got all excited. "I listen to you all the time. I can't believe I'm talking to you," she said. Well, that woman made my day. Unfortunately, immediately when that happens I become very conscious about the impression I'm giving. I mean, if I come across as rude or confused, that's the way they will describe it to their friends and keep that impression for a long time. I can't imagine what it's like for big time, full time celebrities. One bad day and the story that you're a jerk will become part of the pop culture, even if you're not a jerk. I'm sure there are people who will enjoy telling their friends they met you and boy, were you a jerk! It makes someone feel they have real insight into your personal side, even if it isn't true.

HE MEANT SHOOT WITH FILM.
HONEST, HE DID

MY FIRST RADIO job in Bisbee, Arizona in 1977 started at $350.00 a month. Years later I still had this silly idea that it was important to get into a big market. I had come to Wyoming with the help of KRKK/KQSW Operations Manager Chris Alexander Bigelow or air name of Chris Alexander. Three months after I got to Rock Springs, Chris quit and headed to Michigan for a station manager's job in Cadillac. That job in Michigan didn't work out for him so he moved back to his native Chicago area. (I'm getting to the point here, bear with me.) So after I'd spent three years in Wyoming, Chris said I should come to the Chicago area and live with him and his then-wife, (that wasn't what he called her at the time) while I looked for a radio gig in the big city. I thought that was a great opportunity. I wouldn't have to worry about rent and could find something in radio in the third largest market in the country. If that didn't work out I could probably find something at Jewel Foods, one of the largest grocery markets in Chicago.

So almost three years to the day after I arrived in Wyoming, once again my U-Haul and I were on the road. "Hi guys, it's me again. Yeah I'll take the usual size trailer. Can you throw in a hitch this time? It makes it so much easier!" I know what a tree must feel like to be continually transplanted.

I'm a packrat. That character trait certainly doesn't suit the constant traveler. So I tried to buy foam rubber and wicker furniture; you know, the light stuff. Or at least I did do that. Now that I have antiques and some real wood furniture I'm not so anxious to move again. I'm also older and wiser and much more picky about picking up and moving. At least this time I was heading to live with friends. The Bigelows were generous enough to put me up and I was ready to try the adventure. I had scoped out the area on a Thanksgiving visit the previous November. The trees in

Chicagoland were bare; the nuclear winter, as one person once described it, was about to start. Temperatures were in the 60s, so it was actually a pleasant November. The entire experience could have taken a nasty turn considering my buddy Chris perhaps almost got us pummeled by Chicago police. Anyway that's how I see it in hindsight.

On my pre-move visit in November we had gone downtown to Chicago's Michigan Avenue to watch the Christmas Parade. I think it was the intersection of Jackson and Michigan and Chicago's interim Mayor Eugene Sawyer was riding by in an open car. Sawyer took over after the death of Harold Washington. Keep in mind I have my then-film camera with me as usual, and as the parade goes by, my exuberant friend blurts out, "Biff, there's the mayor. Shoot him!" Of course Chris meant with film. Even today I cringe at this. Thanks, Chris, I always wanted to know what it's like to be buried under 1000 pounds of security guards. Fortunately that didn't happen and Chris and I laughedl about it, which is better than paying court costs. Chris, of course, has to talk to friends from a telephone hookup from behind a sheet of glass. Not really. That's a joke and Chris is not doing hard time, last time I checked.

Living in the Chicago suburb of Bolingbrook with my friends the Bigelows, about 30 miles southwest of Chicago, I tried to settle into a new home with a strange town with no job. Ten days later I was back in radio. But, and these are big buts, (I know, it's an old joke) it was only part-time radio at WLTH in Gary, Indiana for essentially minimum wage and (and this is a big and) it was 40 miles one way from Bolingbrook to Gary. I am grateful to Cosmo Currier, then WLTH news director, for "taking me in" as it were. It was a fun crowd to work with.

WLTH is south of downtown Gary. I got lost trying to find it the first time. I was downtown in the parking lot of a fast food place trying to get my bearings. I don't mean this in any disparaging way but it was a new experience for me to stand on a street in a town that is predominantly African American. With every face around, everyone driving by, minority is suddenly a misnomer. I was the different looking one. That's a positive lesson. Probably everybody should feel like a minority now and then. It helps your perspective.

The riverboat casinos came later to Gary and might have brought new life to downtown, but when I worked there, the downtown was in a sad, almost postwar Europe look. It didn't have the bright and peppy atmosphere you might have guessed from Ronnie Howard's song in "The Music Man." However, Gary was also a news happenin' kind of town.

One of my favorite stories WLTH News Director Cosmo Currier told me was the time he sent a reporter to cover a funeral. The guy was so intent on following Cosmo's order to get some "sound" as we say in radio, the reporter, with his microphone, actually straddled the coffin at the gravesite!

As I recall, I've covered only one funeral. It too, was in Gary for WLTH, and was the service for a state senator. Then-Indiana Governor Evan Bayh was there and I briefly stopped him for a comment on the late senator. We were doing live reports and we had to fill time so I ran some of the recording I made of the church music. I don't think there was a lot more I could do. I mean, it's not like the guest of honor will grant an interview. Well, they would if they could, but so would a lot of seemingly lifeless politicians.

Cosmo was big on live reports from car crash scenes, so we did them too. I remember one snowy day on Interstate 80 when some kid tossed a snow-covered rock at a trucker. The trucker stopped his rig, got out and chased the kid and actually caught the troublemaker. Unfortunately for the trucker, the kid and society in general, the mother defended her kid. So there I was, using a cellular phone when cell phones weren't nearly as common, interviewing the trucker from the emergency lane of westbound I-80. So if you drive that stretch between Gary and the Illinois state line, think of me risking my life again in the fast lane.

It's not often I get to interview someone shorter than me. It's also not often (once so far) I've had the chance to interview an authentic 1939 MGM movie "Wizard of Oz" munchkin. Both those opportunities came together at an Oz Festival in northern Indiana.

MEINHARDT RAABE

"As coroner I must aver, I've thoroughly examined her. And she's not only merely dead, she's really most sincerely dead."

For Meinhardt Raabe it was a long road, yellow brick or otherwise, to Munchkinland. The Wisconsin farm dweller had become the Munchkin coroner for the 1939 classic film, "Wizard of Oz." Raabe happily remembered his first impression of Munchkinland and his first steps into the building "and to see all the scenery, the beautiful flowers, the little thatched huts…it blew my mind, so to speak." Coming from his farm to a studio "with all of this beautiful scenery -- well it just was fantastic."

It may have looked like a fantasy in the Land of Oz but, as it can, real life intruded. When we talked in 1989 Raabe said the workday in 1938 was a little longer than what most people were used to. "We were on the set at six o'clock in the morning for makeup, seven o'clock to (the) costume department, eight o'clock ready for shooting and we shoot through 'til six o'clock at night, then back to makeup to have all the extra stuff taken off, then...back to (the) costume department to drop off our costumes and it was eight o'clock at night before we got to eat."

As coroner of Munchkinland, it was Raabe's duty to officially pronounce the Wicked Witch of the East dead, crushed by Dorothy's falling house. It's an integral part of the Munchkin dialogue. "As coroner I must aver, I've thoroughly examined her and she's not only merely dead, she's really most sincerely dead." Raabe got the part after the casting director "in his intuition" picked out certain people for certain parts. For instance, said Raabe, "the three little Lullaby League girls were the only ones that had ever had toe dancing lessons," so he said the three automatically became the Lullaby League. He said, "the Lollipop boys were three fellows all the same size. They had all costumes basically alike and then he lined up about eight fellows to say the lines of the coroner." Raabe said he had been doing a bit of public speaking, "so probably I enunciated a little bit more distinctly than some of the others, so the casting director said, 'okay, you're the coroner.'"

Raabe told me he absolutely enjoyed watching the film. He said, "it's particularly meaningful because, stop and think. How many people have the opportunity of seeing friends of 50 years ago in action?"

The movie credits list the Singer Midgets, certainly a politically incorrect name today, but Raabe wasn't one of that group. "I was an independent." Raabe had already been working with hot dog maker Oscar Mayer, and in fact, was the Oscar Meyer weanie man for 30 years and did their television commercials. To the public he was an actor. To the company he says, "I was a salesman."

Raabe denied any stories that the Munchkins were treated badly. "As far as I'm concerned there was never any problem at the set because (Director) Victor Fleming was very considerate of the Little People. Instead of yelling...you know he'd say 'well now, let's try it this way.' He would just very gently suggest a little bit change in, you know, in action... So we thought he was very, very fine."

At the time we talked, Raabe said children not only enjoyed the film but could repeat every line from it verbatim. The magic of Oz has expanded since then and has even gone into cyberspace. The Yellow Brick Road has traveled farther than even Dorothy Gale from Kansas could have imagined.

Meinhardt Raabe left Oz for good in 2015 when he died at the age of 94, though his character and that of the others in the film live on for generations to enjoy.

Raabe knew about big time movie musicals. Martha Reeves knew about big time music -- rock and roll music so popular it's still a dominant force decades after its creation. Reeves was coming to Chicagoland, I now worked at an oldies station way, way outside Chicago and of course being a good promoter, she talked to our station and fortunately, the interview fell to me.

MARTHA REEVES

"Vandella is a word derived after you're told if you don't get a name in 15 or 20 minutes you're gonna' be called anything."

Martha Reeves' pop image as the leader of the '60s singing group the Vandellas didn't come about by accident. In our 1990 interview Reeves told me, "we were tutored, we were trained, we had choreography lessons, we had chaperones, believe it or not. We had women that went on the road to teach us a lot of the protocols, how to handle ourselves and to make sure we didn't get into any real trouble. Some of us were underage. I happened to be 21, thank God." However, she was still "subjected to the scrutiny of the company." Reeves said, "they fed and guided us and I'm sure a lot of us needed it 'cause we were all rank amateurs and had no idea what we were gonna' do in life, so I think it was a good idea that they did that."

One area where the control was strict was in the phrasing of the songs. But Reeves was grateful that when she came to Berry Gordy's Motown operation she had talent and "I had already recorded so it wasn't like they had to teach me anything." She said, in fact, "I had a lot of liberty, the freedom in my recording." For instance, "Dancing In the Street" was a song that Marvin Gaye had sung but she didn't like the way he sang it, and Reeves said Gaye didn't either. "He didn't want to put it out on himself so I asked him if I could take the song and sing it the way I felt it." Reeves came up with a counter melody to what they gave her and "it turned out to be a winner." Mick Jagger did a "cover," or remake recording of the song and she loved the version he made. "I think it's brilliant because it not only introduced a lot of (Rolling Stones) fans to (the Vandellas) music but it's got audiences worldwide singing the lyrics right along with me, Mick Jagger style. It's great, ya' know. I'm loving this."

Generally she told me she liked covers of old songs because covers, as Reeves put it, "keep the old music alive and I'm always delighted when I hear someone cover our music in particular. It's like a letter saying, 'we dig you.'"

In our 1990 interview, Reeves told me there were people in the music industry without any background, training or talent. "They're into fads and gadgets and gimmicks and synthesized things. Those songs I don't think will have the longevity that the Motown sound has." She felt you have to have some "real people on the sessions."

Reeves said her music "typifies the personalities that Motown had on hand." She had new music to offer in concerts but she added, "people don't really want to hear new stuff from me, for some reason." She said nostalgia is so alive thanks to radio stations, that, at least at the time we talked, "play our music on a daily basis. Our music is as current as anybody in Top 40, Top 10."

Maybe a singer with a popular song can get pretty tired of that song after decades of singing it for audiences. That wasn't the case with Martha Reeves. She strongly rejected any notion that she was tired of hearing requests for any particular song. "Oh no...one of my favorite things is singing. I don't think anything else comes up to that with me as far as excitement and love and enthusiasm." When we talked, Reeves was anxious to get back on the road. Road trips changed for her from the rock and roll days, though. Her first tour with the Vandellas was on a bus with Mary Wells, Marvin Gaye, Stevie Wonder, the Miracles, the Marvelettes, the Contours and a 12-piece band. How's that for a lineup? But Reeves said, "that was one of the most crowded situations. You couldn't really lie down. You had to sit next to somebody that you were cool with, you know, so you could ride for hours and hours." The tour had 94 one-nighters and understandably she was glad show business wasn't like that anymore. She had reached a point in her career where they could travel at their leisure and were very well received. She said they could arrive at a city and didn't have to introduce themselves since they were meeting friends they'd met again and again, and said it was "a real thrill."

When we did the interview she told me their new audience consisted of four generations. "We've got the children who know our music, we've got teenagers who are into rap but they still dig oldies/goodies because their older brothers or mothers and fathers played the music." She added, "my generation, who used to be hippies, can now afford to come to engagements and reminisce and the nostalgia is so great and dear, especially when you can relate to someone in the audience who was there when the record hit. You know what I mean?" There were also older people who encouraged them who also came to their performances, making about four generations. That lineage probably expanded through the years.

Back when the Vandellas played what she called a "theater circuit" they played the Apollo in New York, the Regal Theater in Chicago and others. You'd be at one theater seven days, five or six shows a day with a chance to meet the public and she said maybe even socialize in the city and develop friendships.

On one tour, after they had done six shows, they returned to Detroit and cut the entire "Heat Wave" album, including "My Boyfriend's Back" and "Danke Schoen" in one night. Then with maybe only a nap on the flight, the group went to Baltimore and did five more shows each day. She laughed when she said, "we worked hard." Reeves adds, "that was a hard time, but I enjoyed it."

Reeves noted at the time of our interview there wasn't the urgency, perhaps, to put out an album as there was when Motown was starting, but back then "Heat Wave" was a top ten and they badly needed an album to follow. She added, "it was a crowded stable." Reeves pointed out there was competition to give your finest work. "Motown had other acts so when it was your turn you had to get in there and put your best foot forward and give it your best, come up with a winner."

She described the atmosphere at the old Motown studios as a "beehive." In the office "you might have one guy at the piano with the one artist and another guy…sitting at the table writing lyrics down," and someone else standing at the door arranging. People like Smokey Robinson and Lamont Dozier and brothers Brian and Eddie Holland were writers. "Stevie Wonder came regularly every day to practice and get his act together," and Reeves agreed it was a very creative and rich environment. The situation back then was different for the acts. If you couldn't compete on a local level, "you didn't make it to the pros." Reeves said they competed with the members of the Temptations and the Supremes on a local level. She credits Berry Gordy and others with being smart enough to go around Detroit and gather all the local winners.

My guess is that she must have been asked a thousand times where they came up with the name Vandellas. I made it 1001, discovering the name came from several sources. Part of it came from the name of a street Reeves lived near named Van Dyke, part of it came from her sister's name, a group name they had been using, and some of it came from a woman Reeves held in high regard. "I admired Della Reese, idolize her. I had seen her at New Liberty Baptist Church about a week before I saw her on television singing her hit, "Don't You Know?" and her name is Reese…so I thought if she made it, maybe I could. She gave me incentive. She inspired me. So I used her name in our name." There was pressure to come up with at least something, some name. A record was ready to go and Reeves said, "Vandella is a word derived after you're told if you don't get a name in 15 or 20 minutes you're gonna' be called anything."

In 1990 Reeves had not felt she had reached her peak, her "utopia" as she put it. That energy perhaps also led her in 2005 to devote some time as an elected member of the Detroit City Council. When we talked she felt she had some big recordings in store. The brief time I spoke with Martha Reeves showcased someone in love with music and her professional life.

KEEP THAT ENGINE REVVIN'

MY SUCCESS IN IllNOIS hadn't been stellar so I returned home to Tempe, Arizona. I finally got around to getting my Arizona auto license tags and that day came home to find what some may see as a siren call -- what others may see as a warning siren. WJOL in Joliet, outside Chicago, had a job opening. Did I want to apply? I was leery and this was not an easy decision. I wasn't thrilled to be doing my makeshift job in Arizona taking hotel phone reservations. I wanted to be back in radio. I hate moving and uprooting myself, but I also hate flunkie jobs. You probably do too, I'm sure, but I wanted to be in radio. It seemed when you apply for a job everyone else wants to be in radio too. Other than that it's a small circle, until there's an opening somewhere. Then hundreds of thousands apply. Okay, that's an exaggeration. Maybe tens of thousands. Anyway, I hated working weekends when I was in radio but did I mention I wanted to be in radio? Oh the agony, oh the humanity oh the...okay I took the Joliet job. I just wish they had offered me a job when I applied when I lived just down the road from them, not 1800 miles away. Could have saved me at least that $60.00 in auto tags too, if they had called just 24 hours earlier

So I'm off to Illinois – **again**. I was afraid I was making so many treks across country that gas station owners would start waving at me. This time though, I was not about to hitch up another U-Haul and trudge to Joliet with my stuff only to lose the job and trudge back loaded. With my stuff I mean! Trek, trudge. I had to stop crossing the country, if for no other reason than I was running out of words to describe it. So I put much of my stuff in storage in Tempe. I certainly didn't expect it would be more than four years before I got it out of storage.

On my way east I passed through El Paso, Texas, which as the name implies, you're apparently supposed to do. If you were meant to stop wouldn't it be El Alto? I'm almost sure. So I pull out of El Paso and get a real taste of the size of Texas when I see a sign that says "Dallas, 580 miles." And that wasn't even all the way across the state! I stopped in Dallas to see the JFK assassination related sites. On this trip, without U-Haul, I included Dealey Plaza, the site of the shooting and I added Parkland Hospital and what was called, at the time of the shooting, the Trade Mart, where JFK was scheduled to speak. I also added a stop at Love Field Airport. The JFK assassination has long fascinated me. Now I was in the spots that I had only read about. I couldn't come up with any new revelations about the crime. First rule of a reporter; try not to be 30 years late to the crime scene.

Now back in Illinois, I began work for WJOL AM/WLLI FM in Joliet. I had a regular story beat to cover, as well as whatever happened to come up. The first three days on the job I had already logged 34 hours, another unfortunate sign of the career. However, I did find it was the "whatever comes up" part of the news beat that could be the most interesting part of the job.

I hadn't covered a murder trial since my days in Bisbee. Just never came my way. One day, the regular court beat reporter couldn't be at the trial of a guy charged with shooting five people and killing three of them at a party. The killings were in a studio apartment, of all places. Incidentally, the shooter was later retried and convicted on lesser charges. His lawyer had claimed the shootings were self-defense and that his client feared gang violence.

Anyway, I was sitting in on the trial and they displayed the murder weapon. If you know guns, which I don't, you'd recognize a rectangular body, looking like a small machine gun. This was a good time to remind you and me too to be careful with whom you speak. I turned to the woman sitting on my right in the courtroom and remarked that it was a rather nasty looking weapon. No, not really, she disagreed. I found out she was not a disinterested spectator. It was the shooter's mother! Need I say more? Well, certainly not to her.

If you've never been to a trial of very serious consequence, you should go. You may find it gripping! It can be as fascinating as any TV drama. Yet when you watch TV drama, it's not the same as sitting in a courtroom where I listened to a real life witness testify how she pleaded with the victim not to die. The photo of the face of a dead victim holds a sadness and finality, unlike a "true crime" drama on television.

At the sentencing hearing for a man who killed and cut up his wife and then tried to throw the wrapped body parts in a dumpster, you get a behind-the-scenes feel for the tragedy. You see firsthand how it affects others in the courthouse who are tied to the life and death of the victim. The sense of sadness comes to mind again. It may be high drama on television. It's low down and dirty reality in court. You can't grab a remote control and move to a hair color commercial and turn to a situation comedy. Enough lecturing. If you send me the plane fare, I'll be glad to stand in your living room and repeat this.

If you think lawyers are always the smooth talkers you see on TV shows like "Law & Order" or "Perry Mason" think again. Lawyers may stammer, speak incorrectly and ask to strike a question. It's not in a script.

Speaking of TV versus reality, how many times have you watched a scene of a defendant led to a jail or court covering their face from reporters and public? The only time I saw that in person was in Morris, Illinois, about 60 miles from Chicago. This was after I worked for that Morris radio station that fired me and caused me to return to Arizona. But of course now I was back in Ilinois with WJOL and drove down to Grundy County for this story. Grundy County deputies were leading murder suspect Edward Moore to jail after bringing him back from New York. He was later convicted of murdering and raping a woman and setting her on fire while she was still alive. I tried to ask him a question, even though he was walking along the sidewalk with his face covered by his red plaid shirt. I probably asked it too timidly, although even if he did hear me he probably wouldn't have answered. There's quite a difference between something like that, experiencing it, and only seeing it on a TV screen. Maybe it's the difference between eating a steak and seeing a photo of a steak. In this case, however, I hope I never see it from Edward Moore's perspective. Moore was sent to Death Row.

I oppose the death penalty, even in heinous cases like that and I turned down the opportunity to witness an execution in Illinois. They were conducted at Stateville Correctional Center, in Crest Hill, only about ten miles from where I lived. Every time an execution was planned, the Department of Corrections sent out media notices asking if we wanted to be in the lottery to choose the media witnesses. No, thank you. I don't want that in my mental memory bank. Just driving past the prison was distressing enough. I don't know how many people even think about it as they drive by the institution, but what a place of sorrow it must be, just a few hundred yards across the pretty park-like setting to the high stone walls and office building. Though Stateville is sometimes mistakenly said to be in Joliet, it's in neighboring Crest Hill and it's not the same facility where John Belushi filmed the release scene in "Blues Brothers." That smaller, now former prison, actually is in Joliet.

I would have liked to have interviewed Stateville inmate Richard Speck. He was the maniac who killed eight nurses in Chicago in the 1960s. Though I suppose in his late 40s he probably wouldn't have said much more if anything about the case.

A younger and older mass killer Richard Speck

The closest our paths came to crossing was when he died at Joliet's Silver Cross Hospital across the street from WJOL where I was working. He had been taken there from Stateville Prison, also the site of executions including the execution of serial killer John Wayne Gacy. I wasn't at the radio station when Speck had his heart attack but learned the news when I came in. Some reporter pointed out the irony that Speck died surrounded by nurses.

I did go to a press conference after his death. It was held at the warden's office at Stateville Prison. Entering the facility, they check out what you're carrying before you even get to the warden's office. I was in the office with other reporters from Chicagoland media and as the press conference was going on, I was scrounging around in my recorder bag and found I had forgotten to take out my official Barry Goldwater Senate (and metal) letter opener that I had since my Bisbee days. I'm glad that didn't cause problems going out. They didn't search us again. I actually did forget it was there. Honest.

During the press conference I asked the warden about Speck. I wanted to know if the warden didn't know what Speck had done, would he have liked him? I wish I could have gained some insight into that, but unfortunately the warden said he couldn't like any inmate who was in Stateville. I wish he had given a little more thought to the question. I might have gotten a more revealing answer about Speck rather than about the warden.

DANGER IS MY MIDDLE NAME.
AVOID IS MY FIRST NAME

I DIDN'T OFTEN put myself in danger to cover a story. Even if there were some danger, usually there were enough official types around to watch out for me. Like the time in Yuma, Arizona when I suited up in the firefighter's "turnout" with air bottle and joined another firefighter. Well, saying another firefighter sounds like I was one too. Okay, correction; one firefighter and me, both properly suited up inside the concrete "burn building." The stack of old furniture was set on fire and the room quickly filled with smoke. It did teach me how fast smoke can obscure your vision. If you're in a hotel room, before you go to bed, memorize the exits, because my guess is that by the time a fire awakens you, you won't be able to see and you probably will have to feel your way out. Scary huh? Particularly considering the room will very quickly become twice as hot as your Thanksgiving oven and you won't look as brown and tasty.

One time in Rock Springs, Wyoming, a tanker truck caught fire on the ramp to Interstate 80. Once again there were official types to guard those around the area. Police Commander Glenn Grymes was escorting us to the scene in a squad car. They do that for a few reasons, I think. One is to protect you and that's a big one. They don't want another victim and I guess would like to avoid a lawsuit. They also want to protect the scene for evidence. Regardless of the reasons, they keep an eye on you.

As long as I'm digressing, another time I traveled to a forest fire, north of Rock Springs. I had hoped for a great photo. I could see it clearly in my mind. There I would be, interviewing someone, and the flames leaping behind me. Yeah, right, as if I could get that close. Too many people watch out for you.

I suppose if I became a war correspondent or traveled the globe waiting for chemical plant explosions, I could get some dramatic interviews and photos, but for the most part I have to rely on more mundane settings. I do have that photo of me conducting an interview and behind me is 1800s Oregon Trail graffiti, but you can't blame me for thinking a photo with flames would be nice too. I admit I was a little nervous back in Yuma, Arizona about practice tossing the U.S. Marine Corp Drill Team rifle with the bayonet, but I did it and didn't lose a toe, and I did get a good photo of it from someone with us. For a novice whose rifle was roughly my height, I think I did fairly well.

But back to Illinois. I was driving the WJOL company vehicle looking to report on tornado damage as the tornado sirens were blaring. Sometimes radio was a job I'd pay to do (don't ever repeat that) but it is not a job worth dying for. Come to think of it, I don't know of any job that fits that category, do you?

They talk about news reporting hardening your outlook. I think that happened to me on a small scale. For example, a traffic fatality is a crushing blow to the family, a terrible tragedy. I know that, intellectually and emotionally. However, I was always looking for ways to fill out a newscast with a dramatic lead story.

That may sound cold and I think I'm a long way from a cold person. But you get in a mindset that's detached and yet still focused on your job. Yet I am also aware of the effect of a story once it's "out there." Take a preachy tone about a weird crash with odd circumstances and you'll hear about it. If someone does something stupid with a firecracker, it may be a funny story for you to tell. "Did you hear about the guy who, etc." But take that tone on the air with a serious story and you might hear about it from the victim's relative, and honestly, you'd deserve to hear about it.

Once I got a story from county police about a kid who was given a "candle" by a neighbor and tried to light it, finding out the hard way that it was what's called a "quarter stick" of dynamite. It may be grocery store conversation to you, but it's a sad, dramatic, painful story for someone and they deserve to be treated decently on the air.

I know a story about a teacher strike will be heard on the air and interpreted as favorable, unfavorable or fair and neutral depending on the listener. Hopefully, the last option is the one they'll choose but we're talking high emotion in a story like that. However, a Joliet Junior College teachers' strike was underway and I went to the picket line. I was met with excitement. I really believe some people think that because you're covering a story, you're on their side. Or maybe they were just glad to get some coverage.

I once attended a seminar in Los Angeles that covered radio and TV, though more emphasis on TV. The seminar included some notables in the broadcasting business. Contacts are probably a big part of any career but as I've mentioned, surprisingly radio is not that big a circle, until there's a job opening. Then it seems there are, in the words of Carl Sagan, "billions and billions" of us. Of course, when one of us in the business jumps off the merry-go-round, for example to go into public relations, as many of us do, we all shift to the right, in the available musical job chairs. I have to clarify the "shift to the right" thing. Maybe you wouldn't believe any reporter shifted to the right, politically. The popular image has us left of Joseph Stalin. Frankly what is left of Stalin's image? Maybe you'd be surprised to find a Libertarian such as myself in the biz. Fiscally conservative and socially liberal best describes where I stand but those definitions and labels shift, so it can be hard to pin down, even though the principles remain.

I really think my Libertarian views have helped me be more objective in my reporting. I don't automatically accept either major party line or assumption. But then, I like to think I don't automatically accept any idea.

If you're a Baby Boomer you know about Wolfman Jack. The famous howl was a staple of rock and roll for many years. As it often did, a new book brought an author to my doorstep. The wonderful part is that this time the author was the Wolfman. The sad part is that his book promotion was the last event of his life. I was a part of those last ten days.

WOLFMAN JACK

"They looked like nice folks and all of a sudden there's several people just wanting to make love to me."

All I knew about the Wolfman was the public image. There was the outlandish TV and radio character and thanks to the movie "American Graffiti," a screen personality. So when the chance came to interview Wolfman Jack, I looked forward to finding out about the man behind the hair and the howl. What I didn't know as he talked about his life philosophy and his Wolfman persona, was that he was summing up a life that would end ten days later. On July 1, 1995, Wolfman Jack had just returned to his North Carolina home after the promotion of his new book, when he died of a heart attack at age 57. Ten days earlier, on June 21, I was working at WJOL in Joliet and preparing to begin our phone interview. Before we got underway Wolfman asked if I were near the prison. A prison is a common connection with the public's image of Joliet. He said, "it must be an evil presence over there, man." When I began our talk by referring to him with his real name of Bob Smith, he quickly corrected me. "No, don't use that name." He made it clear he wanted to be called Wolfman Jack.

Wolfman was in the middle of a book promotion tour for "Have Mercy! Confessions of the Original Rock 'N' Roll Animal." "It's all about a guy who comes from Brooklyn, New York, who didn't have nothin' to start with," said Wolfman, "and I managed to do the right thing...because when you do right, you come out right, ya' know?"

Wolfman's words about his abuses of his physical well-being seem ironic when you think of the fate that was just days away. However, Wolfman said drug use was fashionable into the early '80s, and "if you had any brains at all, by the time you reached about 1982... you had given it all up and you're getting yourself back in the good health again and trying to make your life last a little bit longer, ya' know?" That's where he said he was when we talked in '95. He said, "I mean, I went through it, I enjoyed it, I'm not ashamed of it." At least he avoided one problem. Wolfman told me he never was a drinker. It only took one drink to make him sick. "So that's the thing that probably saved me. The other stuff was easy to give up."

Wolfman got the most enjoyment from "being in the happiness business and being able to bring a lot of good time rhythm and blues to these folks out there, and ease their ills with all that good music." Wolfman said he'd learned "the only way to be a success in life is to go out of your way and really try to do things for people to make 'em happy when it's unexpected. Maybe not right away, but it will always come back to you. So selfishly, I've always tried to do for other people."

Wolfman Jack helped make a name for himself early in his career at a 250,000-watt Mexican radio station. That's five, count 'em five, times as powerful as any U.S. AM radio station. The station was near the U.S. border and sent his gravelly voice into a big chunk of the U.S. "Wolf" hosted the live television show, "Midnight Special" in 1973, and George Lucas gave him the chance to play himself in the movie "American Graffiti" with Ron Howard, Richard Dreyfuss and Harrison Ford.

How much of his personality was the Wolfman and how much was just Bob Smith? Would he have been the same if you had met him in a grocery store? Bob "Wolfman Jack" Smith told me, "oh yeah...I've been doin' Wolfman Jack now for 34 years, man. I mean, after a certain period of time you become the character. I think we all become characters, especially if you're an entertainer. You create an image for yourself and...if it works for you, you improve upon it and you do the best you can."

Can you picture Wolfman Jack as a Fuller Brush salesman? Yeah, me either, but it happened. Imagine him showing up at your door. Of course in those days he was just Bob Smith. "Boy, I ran into some real weird situations doin' that man, knockin' on people's doors. You don't know what you're gonna' walk into." One time he showed up at a woman's door with her free gift he offered as a Fuller Brush salesman. The woman and her friends invited him in. "I was just a young fella," said Wolfman. "They looked like nice folks and all of a sudden there's several people just wanting to make love to me. It was just an unbelievable experience."

His career seemed back on track with his book and syndicated radio show he was hosting called "Live From Planet Hollywood," out of Washington, DC.

He wrapped up our interview saying, "the old Wolfman's back in the saddle again, Biff." A heart attack July 1, 1995 knocked him out of the saddle, but his story remains and so does the memory of his howl.

CAN YOU AT LEAST WAIT UNTIL MY PHONE IS INSTALLED BEFORE YOU FIRE ME?

IF YOU HAVEN'T been fired, you haven't had a career in radio. Ask almost any radio veteran and you'll probably see them nod their head. I've worked at more than one dozen stations and have been fired or laid off several times. This isn't easy for someone like me who doesn't even like to be yelled at. But look at the circumstances. You're often working for small mom and pop shops or small time managers for wealthy owners or new owners who want their own special sound on the air or are insecure and don't know what they want, but they don't know radio, or you have transient managers who are more concerned about short term gain than long term investment. Or maybe it's just Tuesday. I've met some of the most insecure people. That's a problem when they're in a position of power. The money people and the creative types will often differ, but hopefully the clash is minor.

There was one time I recall when sale of airtime dictated news coverage, though certainly one time is one too many. It happened when I was at WJOL in Joliet, under the ownership of former Will County Coroner Robert Tezak. Incidentally, Tezak later went to prison for paying someone to burn down a bowling alley he owned and being involved in burning a building that housed some federal records. Someone questioned why somebody with Tezak's millions would want to collect the insurance on a bowling alley. That's probably an easy answer. The attraction is surely one more million.

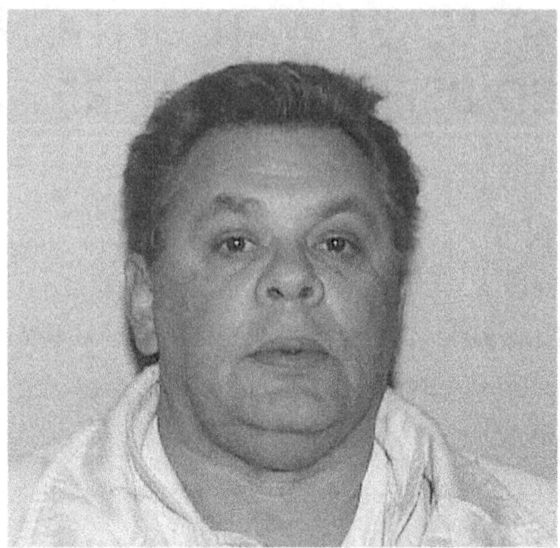

One time noted local Joliet and Will County figure, businessman, elected official and convicted felon Robert Tezak

I heard, but didn't confirm one part of the story, that Tezak wasn't pleased with the amount of damage done by the fire, so he asked for some of his arson-for-hire money back. But, that's a side story and again I digress. Back to the news/sales quandary. The WJOL station manager came to the newsroom and wanted a story done on a home building-supply chain store grand opening. We were told they spent a lot of money on advertising. That certainly makes it newsworthy right? Wrong. That certainly means we do the story, right? Right. Well, I got assigned the story. I tried to give it as much news angle as I could, rather than making it sound like a commercial for the business. But pressure like that leaves a really bad taste in your mouth. (Here I am years later still talking about it.) I don't know how the news director reacted when he heard the manager's "request," but I know he was a strong company man, and I know I had to do the story. This is the same news director who sided with the "company line" one day when the tornado warning sounded. You'll love this. Everyone at the station was heading for the basement, including the operations manager/engineer. Another reporter and I decided to stay upstairs in the newsroom. But we were also worried about the danger of flying glass from the windows. So Janet and I sat on the floor, still in the newsroom, but a little safer. Later we caught flak from this operations manager and through him to the news director, not because they were concerned about our safety. Oh no. Then why? Because we looked like we were slacking off! Can you believe that? That's the true definition of a radio weasel. The news director was all too happy to follow the company line, too. Amazing. Weasels, weasels everywhere.

That's why it's so important to really love the business or at least have a love-hate relationship. You've read as I ranted about the downside. You've also read about the love of radio. Fortunately love can be stronger than hate. For me, the "frosting on the cake" can be those fun and noteworthy interviews, including pop culture legends such as Sonny Bono.

SONNY BONO

"I wrote ten gold records and I produced a top three television show and now I'm standing here being bawled out by a midget."

In June 1996, Sonny Bono was a relatively new U.S. congressman and less than two years away from the skiing accident that would take his life. When we talked at a press conference, Bono was campaigning for a local congressman, helping him raise money. If the words, "Congressman Sonny Bono" seemed like a contradiction to you, it was also an attitude Bono knew was out there. He told me, "a lot of people didn't know what to expect frankly, and I think that a lot of people thought 'what's this world coming to?' when I got elected." He found his celebrity status in show business both a help and a hindrance in his new career in Washington. "It's a double edged sword," he said. "You go there, you're a straight man, so people sometimes think you're gonna' be the person they see on television and if you're a straight man, if you're not Charleton Heston, then you don't get to be Moses, so you're a guy that takes the shots." But Bono said, "I'm very friendly with everybody and I try to get along with everybody and I think that sort of dissipated as an issue, but when I first got there it was apparently an issue. So part of it was very good, 'cause you're known, but then the other part of it is you're also a target."

When it comes to phonies, Bono found some differences between Hollywood and Washington. In Hollywood, he told me, "we know that some people are gonna' come there and try to run a game and don't have the ability to pull it off and they're 'spottable.' But I think in Congress that isn't as apparent." However, Bono found show business and government very similar, "as far as attitudes, as far as it being a power source and how you perform in that power source -- whether it goes to your head and you become arrogant and just thrive on getting known and not thrive on getting things done."

After our press conference, the reporters were allowed to have a picture taken with him. Professionally, I was reluctant, since it really steps across the objectivity line, but what the heck, would you pass up a chance to have your picture taken with Sonny Bono? I mean, this is Sonny "I Got You Babe," "The Beat Goes On," Cher's ex-husband, Bono.

I pointed out to him I wasn't wearing a suit (as he and the other congressman were) but he told me that wasn't his favorite form of dress either. Someone later suggested that maybe bellbottoms would have been more in line. I wish I'd thought to suggest that to him. Though it's awkward to have a photo taken with someone you interview, I now treasure the picture, particularly considering he left this world just a year and a half later.

After our press conference and photo time, Bono went downstairs to address a crowd of supporters of the local Republican congressman, though my guess is some in the crowd weren't necessarily Republicans and wouldn't have cared if Bono were a member of the American Bathtub Users Party as long as they got the chance to see this '60s pop culture icon. Bono told the crowd he was "about the most unpolitical politician you're ever gonna' meet." He said he was a congressman, "but I'm not a politician." He explained he had expected to spend his days running a restaurant, "cook some pasta and raise a couple more kids." What actually happened was after he "broke up with that woman," meaning Cher of course, he wasn't at all prepared. "I thought I was gonna' be in show business all my life and that's all I wanted to do." When that ended he was as shocked as anyone and compared it to losing his right arm. Even though he wanted to stay in show business, Bono said people he used to call "weren't in, anymore."

When a celebrity's career is waning, Bono said "what a lot of us do is become professional guest stars." "I hold the record for the most "Fantasy Islands." Since he wasn't singing and dancing anymore Bono decided to become an actor and get his own show. By the way, he said the TV show's "Fantasy Island" wasn't an island. "It's sort of a dirty lot in Burbank with fake palm trees." Bono felt stuck. If he stopped show business, people would know he wasn't a star anymore. "They already knew I wasn't a star anymore." He was trying to decide what he was going to do and figured it would be too embarrassing to leave show business, so he was taking the guest star roles. One day Bono was doing his "umpteenth" "Fantasy Island" appearance and his head was not in it. It was tedious. As he put it, "you'd go out and say your line, then go back and you'd sit in the trailer for a week." So he had a scene with diminutive Herve Villechaize, the man who played the character "Tattoo." Bono was supposed to deliver the line, "it's a beautiful day out today, Tattoo." Instead, Bono said "it's a beautiful day out today, Pontoon." Villechaize got mad, but Bono got something else -- a revelation. Bono said Villechaize "was bawling me out for calling him Pontoon," and upset for not recognizing him as the star of the show. Bono said he was looking down at Herve "and (Herve) kept going, and I was just watching, and I thought, you know, 'I wrote ten gold records and I produced a top three television show and now I'm standing here being bawled out by a midget.'" That's when Bono decided to get out of show business. He told himself, "thanks God, I'm outta' here." It's not a politically correct story talking about Little People like that, but Bono warned us he was not a politician.

He planned to retire in Palm Springs with his wife when suddenly "bureaucracy" came into his life. Maybe I should say pounced. It wasn't something Bono was used to dealing with. "When you're in show business, somebody does something for you all the time, so you don't have to do it."

After buying a restaurant in Palm Springs, Bono decided to take 15 minutes off and go down to city hall to get a sign permit for his restaurant. That's when he found out it doesn't quite work that way. He was told he would have to follow procedures and policy to get the permit and told to fill out the papers and bring them back. He also had plans to remodel his house, so while he was still at city hall he turned to the other counter, doing what Bono called his "penalty time" at that counter and the same guy came around to help him. Bono figured, "well that's good, we're old friends now." Bono adds, "and he didn't recognize me." Bono was told to fill out the forms and bring them back. "This went on for weeks and for months," and he couldn't figure out what was so complicated about getting a couple of permits. Finally he decided to start on the house, figuring when he got his permits he'd already be along in the process. That's when he learned another lesson about government. He said, "up until then I thought only one guy worked at city hall, but several people worked at city hall and they were in my front yard," asking Bono what he was doing. They gave him a red tag. "I didn't know what a red tag was, but a red tag means stop doing whatever you're doing or they will kill you." Bono reminded his audience he had no plan to go into government. Finally he told the official not to worry about the permits and that it wasn't a problem. The official told Bono he had to have the permits and they had to give them to him. Bono told them not to worry about it, because, in Bono's words, "I'm going to run for mayor and fire you." That's when he says he became a politician. But Bono added, "I'm not entirely heartless. Dave is now my gardener."

Salvatore Philip Bono was 62 years old when he was killed skiing at South Lake Tahoe, California, on January 5, 1998. On his gravestone, it reads "And the beat goes on."

Pop culture figures seem to come around fairly often thanks to the trend to nostalgia. Peter Noone didn't have the political resume Sonny Bono did and didn't have the show business variety in his background. But Peter Noone had one thing Sonny didn't – Herman's Hermits.

PETER "HERMAN" NOONE

"Somebody thought I looked like Sherman, but we thought his name was Herman and I became Herman."

Peter Noone has an up close and personal relationship with Henry the VIII and there aren't too many of us who can say that. But what else would you expect from the man who sang "I'm Henry (or "Enery") the VIII, I am?" Peter Noone is better known, perhaps, as Herman of the '60s pop group, Herman's Hermits. In 1992, Noone was on the concert circuit and I asked him if he'd ever stopped to count how many media interviews he had done. "No, I've never actually stopped to count. That's a good idea," he said. "Let me start now. One, two, three, six. No I'm not going to count now." I suggested there had been thousands. "Well, you know, if people stop asking you questions, it means nobody's interested anymore. I don't look forward to that part." Is there one question that annoyed him the most, or the silliest? "There's a bunch of them." He said, "my least favorite one is 'what is your favorite color?'" He said that was a "Sixteen Magazine" kind of question. Since he's British, maybe I should spell that "colour."

Peter, or Herman's audience in the 1990s was different from his concert fans of the 1960s. "In the 60s the audience were all 12" and he says "they had their mothers with them. Now it's mothers and daughters who are 18, so it's much better now." When we talked in '92, Noone said the same 12-year-olds who were now older were bringing their daughters to the shows and he considered that a good thing. The generations have moved on since that interview and, of course, add up for any long term performer.

Noone agreed the music industry had changed a lot technically, but if the technology around when we talked in the '90s had been around in the '60s he didn't think Herman's Hermits would have sounded different. In '92 when we talked he had just completed a new record. "We went in the studio...and recut like 12 Herman's Hermits songs and two new songs, and we did the whole thing in four days, the whole album recorded and mixed in four days." He added, "I like doing things with the energy of the musicians and the players, you know, rather than technically." Noone said, "my songs are all spiritual songs, and if you get into them you enjoy them, and if you don't, then best leave the studio."

Remember the cartoon from the Rocky and Bullwinkle show with Mr. Peabody the dog and his boy, Sherman? That's where the name Herman's Hermits came from -- sort of. Noone said, "somebody thought I looked like Sherman, but we thought his name was Herman and I became Herman."

Noone wasn't concerned about the way the audience viewed his music of the '60s -- seriously or playfully – as long as they bought the records. "The whole point to make records was to sell 'em. Nowadays people make records for other motives. We wanted to sell lots of records." He said Herman's Hermits was proved right "because we sold more records than anybody, except for the Beatles and the (Rolling) Stones."

As far as a favorite of his old stuff? "I like 'em all. I like "Mrs. Brown, You've Got a Lovely Daughter," I like "Henry the VIII," I like "I'm Into Something Good," I like "Silhouettes." I like a lot of 'em. I like 'em all. I'm pretty silly, really, aren't I?" I asked in our '92 interview if performing were still as much fun for him? "Oh yeah. Well, sometimes it's fun. Today it's been a lot of fun, but we're doing two dates," adding "we're a bit wasted, but once you get onstage you're always okay." At that point something was spilled on his jacket and he worried whether it would be wearable. "The jacket has definitely been wasted hasn't it?" Perhaps at that moment he may have wished he still owned his clothing boutique. "That was great fun. (Jimi) Hendrix used to buy his clothes there and all the guys from the Experience and the Animals and everything. Just a fun thing." Noone had also done some light opera in work by Gilbert and Sullivan. "Sounds light but it was hard work for me."

Noone even worked in the lyrics to one of his songs in a TV situation comedy appearance. So obviously he didn't take the music too seriously. "How can you take it seriously? It's not serious. I'm Henry the VIII I am. Henry the VIII I am, I am. I got married...It's not a serious song. It's a fun song."

I left him at his dressing room trailer where one of his tasks before the show was to find a place to wash his hands. Ah, the joys of working on the road.

Maybe that same joy or frustration was there for Steve Allen. When I talked with him by phone in a couple of interviews over the years, I found an interesting blend of personality -- a very serious side and of course what may be better known, a very comic side.

STEVE ALLEN

"Somebody pointed out awhile back I'm the only comedian in show business who does not have an act."

When Steve Allen worked on stage, he liked to work loose. His stage show included picking 20 or 30 questions from cards from the audience that struck him as particularly funny. He told me, "that's basically my comedy for the night. I've always worked that way." The comedian, talk show host, songwriter, author and actor's work covered decades in show business. He wrote thousands of songs, including "This Could Be the Start of Something Big," dozens of books, produced the Emmy award-winning PBS television show "Meeting of Minds," played the title character in the movie "The Benny Goodman Story," and created perhaps his most memorable product, the "Tonight Show," which he also hosted. That was before Jack Paar, Johnny Carson and Jay Leno and Jimmy Fallon. Allen is also in the TV Academy's Hall of Fame.

With a resume like that, you'd have to have a mind that was regularly on the prowl for ideas. Allen said an active working mind came naturally to him. "It's just automatically the way I work. When it's hot I perspire, when I'm tired I sleep, and when I'm just not occupied with any given activity my brain clicks in and gets me occupied."

The New York native also called Chicago home. He started working around Chicago and one day got a call for a gig as a piano player. He took a streetcar to a neighborhood he didn't know and when he got there the band had started playing. A musician has to be prepared. He could hear them playing polka music, a type of music he didn't know. Jazz is played in different keys than polka and he wasn't ready for the task before him. But he told me, "I learned in about 20 minutes...I was finally somehow doing it." Allen called polka a "happy" music and something he said at the time that he preferred over "a lot of the garbage that passes for popular music today."

One song that Allen wrote, "This Could Be the Start of Something Big," had its beginning partly in a dream, specifically the "title and the main thrust of the melody." He had been assigned to write a musical, and he said, "therefore my brain had obviously gotten to work on it, even though I was busy doing the usual 14 other things too, at the time. The name of the show was 'The Bachelor,' so I had to write a song about a guy who was just having laughs with a lot of different women and didn't want to narrow down on one of them." Allen wanted to write about a man who got the idea that maybe love is better than having a different woman every week. "So that was the idea in my head and suddenly in the dream it all began to fall into place." I think that's pretty good for someone who never learned to read music and always played by ear.

Being known everywhere had it ups and downs, but in our interview Allen said, "the pluses, fortunately, far outnumber the minuses." But there was the problem of privacy. "If you go into a grocery store to buy a toothbrush, you're apt to become involved in four or five conversations you're not looking for. But in most cases the people say very lovely things, so as I say, by and large, it's a plus." I pointed out he probably never had to wait for a restaurant table either. He agreed. "Yeah, that would be one of the pluses too. I always feel a little guilty about that. (Wife, actress) Jayne (Meadows) has more nerve about that. If we walk into a restaurant, she'll go over and talk to the maitre d' or the owner and tell them who's the guy standing in the back of the line, but I'm a little shy about that."

Allen was an interesting combination of comic and almost professor. His serious demeanor came through when he talked in the 1990s about the decline in society. "Our culture is really in a morass of moral decline and garbage," he said. That seemed to be a pretty clear indictment. He also didn't believe there was a link between talent and show biz success. "If ours were a rational planet the most popular people and the wealthiest performers would be those who are most talented. But there seems almost no correlation at all between talent on the one hand and commercial success on the other." He felt there are those who are remarkably gifted, "but you could probably put them all on one small school bus and in contrast you'd have to get a large meeting hall to accommodate all the people who are pretty much getting by on luck and sleeping with the, you know, network executives or whatever the hell they do to get ahead." While he said the public doesn't seem to have much sensitivity to talent, Allen added, "what they are almost morbidly fascinated by is success," and he felt if you create a stir you get known. "Oh yes, have a fistfight with Mick Jagger or get raped by a former Beatle," and Allen said, "you'll be all over the tabloids and probably have four agents wanting to handle you."

Before his TV pioneer days, Allen was in radio and at the time we talked it was still a love for him. But he didn't have any respect for the so-called "shock jocks," which he said had nothing to do with talent. "It's just a way of getting attention. You could probably get just as much attention by marching someone up to the corner of 42nd and Broadway and starting to hit him with a stick. You'd certainly attract a crowd immediately, but I think it's better not to hit people with sticks, whether they're verbal or real."

Allen did the "Tonight Show" for four years. If you love TV history and the tangible connection to entertainment you should probably skip the next sentence. You won't like to learn that a storage clerk who wanted more shelf space got rid of most of the old "Tonight Show" tapes by burning them, forever losing Allen's early work.

He said, "there's some of those nights I would have ordered burned myself, because even good shows are not great every week or every night. But it's a real cultural tragedy that so much of that was lost." Allen said, "one night we had 90 minutes of glorious music because we had the famous composer Richard Rodgers seated at the piano, and occasionally he'd get tired of playing his songs so he'd ask me to sit down and do it, or I would ask (Tonight Show bandleader) Skitch Henderson to take over the piano and we had Andy Williams and Steve Lawrence and Eydie Gorme sitting around the instrument singing Richard Rodgers classics for the whole hour and a half." Allen called that "one of the best things that ever happened on television...because the music is so beautiful." But that tape was burned too. Poet Carl Sandburg did about 90 minutes on the show but sadly that, too, was lost to the flames of expediency.

After more than 50 years in show biz, he didn't feel the need to change a thing. "I've had so much good luck I feel guilty about it all, so if it worked out that well, I would be very ill-advised to start tinkering with it." Steve Allen died in late 2000 at age 78. "The Tonight Show" host Jay Leno gave him an on air tribute praising him for his innovation. The entertainment industry and American culture lost someone who was a trailblazer "at the start of something big."

By 1994 I had moved to yet another station, WKBM south of Joliet in Wilmington, where my talk show allowed me the freedom to track down a lot of significant folks.

One national and global figure who definitely had a reason to be serious was former Astronaut Jim Lovell. He also had a new book out. (See the trend?) So of course I had to follow up and grab an interview, again on the run. I caught up with him (actually I really hate that phrase) at a bookstore signing, and since I had made arrangements the book store coordinator led us back into a small room where I could talk with the man who was almost lost in space.

JAMES LOVELL

"We were the first people to leave the Earth, essentially, and then see the far side of the Moon. The most thrilling flight of course was Apollo 13."

FORMER ASTRONAUT JAMES LOVELL didn't suffer from triskaidekaphobia. An abnormal fear of number 13 was not a problem for the man who made space history and nearly lost his life doing it. Though the number 13 didn't bother him, you could understand if he were a bit leery of the number. Lovell had many accomplishments in space, including commanding Apollo 13, launched from the Cape in Florida on April 11, 1970. Maybe you say, at least that's not April 13? True, but Apollo 13 fired off the pad at 1:13 p.m. Houston time or as they say in military time, 1313. With the command module and the three astronauts on board, connected to the lunar module, the craft rocketed to the moon with the goal of making NASA's and the nation's third lunar touchdown. Two days after the launch, (April 13, by the way) there was an explosion behind the command module in an area that held life sustaining power and oxygen. When that happened, NASA scrubbed the idea of landing on the moon and concentrated on just getting the crew back home alive. Apollo 13 limped around the far side of the Moon and safely returned to Earth by using the attached lunar lander called "Aquarius" as a form of lifeboat, providing power and oxygen. Lovell said the lunar lander "Aquarius" was number seven. "We figure if 13 is a bad number, seven must have been a good number and that got us home." Maybe Lovell didn't have any concern about the number 13, but after the Apollo near-disaster, NASA stopped designating any craft "13."

Lovell was already in the space history books well before Apollo 13. In 1965, in the Gemini two-man capsule space program, Lovell and Frank Borman and their Gemini 7 capsule took part in the Earth orbit rendezvous with a second manned Gemini capsule. Living conditions in those early spacecraft were less than spacious. Lovell described it to me as "14 days in a men's room."

On Gemini 12, in 1966, Lovell and Buzz Aldrin completed the final Gemini flight. Three years later, in 1969, Aldrin would fly on Apollo 11 and become the man who accompanied Neil Armstrong to the surface of the moon in the first lunar landing. However, before the Apollo 11 flight Lovell and Borman again teamed up, adding William Anders in their Apollo 8 spacecraft in December 1968 and became the first humans to travel to the Moon. Apollo 8 wasn't a lunar landing flight of course. For Lovell the flight of Apollo 8 was "the peak as far as experiencing something new." The crew were the first humans to escape the gravity of Earth and see the Moon up close. By reaching and orbiting the Moon, the flight gave Mankind the new perspective of our small blue and white Earth from the distance of the Moon.

At our 1994 interview, Lovell said, "I still look at the Moon and I think my companions do too, saying there have been just a few people that made it to the Moon." Lovell was disappointed his Apollo 13 planned landing on the Moon never happened, "but I was out there...made it out there twice as a matter of fact." Though disappointed, Lovell says the Apollo 13 flight was very successful because they got back safely and avoided almost certain catastrophe. "To me, there was a sense of achievement."

The Tom Hanks movie about the flight of Apollo 13 dramatizes the danger and the crew's struggle to get back to Earth. Maybe you don't know you can see Lovell in a bit part in the movie, playing an officer greeting the returning crew to Earth aboard the recovery ship. In the real Apollo 13 crisis, Lovell's private thoughts centered on the danger and the question of whether they'd get home. The low point was about an hour or two after the explosion, when they didn't know exactly what had happened, but they were losing power and water. He remembered, "we didn't talk too much about it, though. As long as we had something to do, we just kept working to get ourselves home." Lovell discovered something about himself during the crisis. "I learned that I was still calm and cool and collected, which amazed me. People often say, 'did you panic?' I say 'no,' because if we panicked we'd be right back where we started from. So I didn't really panic."

You may remember the 1970 fictional movie where three Apollo-like astronauts are stranded in Earth orbit in their capsule called "Ironman One." The movie, "Marooned" stars Gregory Peck, Richard Crenna and Gene Hackman. One of the three on board the "Ironman One" spacecraft dies in space. For us it was just a movie. Jim Lovell saw it too on the movie screen, at a Houston premiere, three months before his aborted lunar landing. After the real life explosion in space, his wife remembered the similarities and hoped the real life version would have a better outcome. As you know, it did.

Lovell said, "I would have liked to have seen 13 land on the Moon and find some odd thing on the Moon like an ancient...Martian that didn't quite make it to the Earth." But he also feels the satisfaction of a safe return for the crew of Apollo 13.

Lovell, in his 70s at the time, felt young people read about the lunar flights in history books but were very much interested in space flight and the Moon and Mars. As he put it, "there is a fascination about space, regardless of what people say about the practicality about it."

Fred Olivi was a pilot too, also on an historic mission. Both pilots were a major part of their eras. For Lovell it was a mission of manned travel from earth to another body in space, For Olivi it was a mission to end a world war.

FRED OLIVI

"You hear all kinds of stories. A lot of us are in the nuthouse and we're having all kinds of problems. Well that's not true...I've lived a full life and so have the other crews that dropped the two bombs."

Nagasaki atomic bombing mission co-pilot Fred Olivi on my talk show at WKBM Wilmington, Illinois

Retired Lieutenant Colonel Fred Olivi saw something very few Americans have witnessed and hopefully no one will ever see again -- the explosion of an atomic bomb over a city. On August 6, 1945 the B-29 Enola Gay piloted by Colonel Paul Tibbets dropped the world's first atomic bomb on a population. The blast that wiped out Hiroshima, Japan wasn't enough to end the war against Japan and three days later a second atomic bomb was dropped on Nagasaki. Olivi was the 23 year old co-pilot on that second mission, commanded by then-Major Chuck Sweeney aboard the B-29 known as Bockscar. As commander, Sweeney was in the pilot's left seat. The co-pilot was 1st Lieutenant Charles Albury in the right seat and between the two was co-pilot/third pilot 2nd Lieutenant Olivi.

The August 9 mission ended up over Nagasaki, Japan, but I was surprised to learn Nagasaki was not the mission's primary target. The number one target for this second atomic bombing was the Japanese city of Kokura. History can turn on the smallest event and the lives of Kokura residents took a dramatic turn. History spared them, thanks to something as unpredictable as the weather. Olivi said "when we got to Kokura it was about eight-tenths cloud cover and we had orders to drop the bomb visually only. They didn't want us to use radar." That's because the top commanders didn't want to take that chance and the technology wasn't as good as it is today. Bockscar made three runs over Kokura with the hope that bombardier Kermit Beahan could see the drop point through the clouds and drop the bomb visually. They spent 50 minutes trying to do that and then pilot Sweeney decided to head for target two, Nagasaki. The weather over Nagasaki was even worse with nine-tenths cloud cover. There was also a problem with the plane's fuel. Before the flight they discovered they would carry 600 gallons of fuel that because of a bad transfer pump wouldn't be able to be pumped into the wing tanks and into the engines. Enola Gay pilot Tibbets told Bockscar commander Sweeney that those gallons of fuel were designed as a weight balance for the ten thousand pound atomic bomb up in the front bomb bay of the plane. Sweeney made the decision to fly the mission and the crew hoped everything would be okay.

After the time spent over Kokura trying to complete the bomb run and deciding to move on, the crew figured it had enough fuel for one bomb run over Nagasaki and then to fly to the emergency landing site on Okinawa. There was no other backup target, so when they discovered Nagasaki had even more cloud cover than Kokura, rather than going all the way back to Tinian with the bomb and landing at Okinawa, Olivi said it was better to use the best method they had at Nagasaki to drop the weapon. That method was radar.

After the bomb was released from the plane, Olivi and the rest of the crew wanted to see what was happening below. "We all looked down and we see the entire city was covered with smoke and dust and fires breaking out all over the area, and we watched the mushroom cloud come out of the center." You've probably seen the picture of that mushroom cloud. Olivi saw it in person. "We were all concentrating down below and nobody was paying attention to the mushroom cloud." Scientists had told them the cloud was radioactive and getting engulfed in it would have given them radiation poisoning and would eventually kill them. Olivi remembers, "all of a sudden one of the crewmembers in the back hollered 'the mushroom cloud is coming toward us.' Well, we didn't want this to happen to us so... Sweeney put the aircraft down into a dive and to the right full throttle and I remember looking out the window...and I couldn't tell for a while whether we were gaining on the cloud or the cloud was gaining on us, but finally we did pull away, because if we didn't I wouldn't be here telling the story." The plane was to the side of the cloud because the atomic mushroom had already risen past the B-29's altitude of 30,000 feet and the cloud continued rising to 50,000 or 60,000 feet.

The crew of Bockscar felt three concussions after the bomb exploded. "The first was the worst," said Olivi, "and that shook the aircraft up pretty thoroughly and the scientists had warned us about this, but we were hoping we weren't going to be structurally damaged so we'd have to have a forced landing or forced to ditch and get picked up by the Japanese." Shortly after that first really rough blast "we got another shock blast of lesser intensity." Finally, the plane was hit with a third concussion that was the least forceful of the three. Flying at 30,000 feet altitude, the crew didn't hear anything and there wasn't any smell from the blast, but decades later the sight was still vivid in Olivi's memory. "Inside this mushroom cloud was like a boiling caldron," and Olivi said it had a myriad of colors, in fact, "all colors of the rainbow." The other thing that stuck in his mind "was the salmon colored pink and that's the predominant color that I still remember." Olivi said on the earlier Enola Gay B-29 mission over Hiroshima, pilot Tibbets reported he could taste the lead fillings in his teeth, but Olivi said, "none of us experienced that sort of a situation, as far as I know, on our crew."

Before the two atomic bombing flights, Olivi and the rest of the crewmembers had been given the option of backing out of the missions. "They told us exactly what they expected the bomb to do." He said the choice was theirs. Colonel Tibbets told the two crews, one for the

Hiroshima flight and one crew, including Olivi, that would fly the second atomic bombing mission on Bockscar, that because a lot of civilians would be killed by the bombs, if anyone wanted to get out of the missions all they had to do was step down and be replaced and there wouldn't be any action taken against them.

One misconception Olivi often heard and was surprised by is the story that most of the atomic bomb flight crew went crazy. Olivi denied that. "You hear all kinds of stories. A lot of us are in the nuthouse and we're having all kinds of problems. Well that's not true...I've lived a full life and so have the other crews that dropped the two bombs." He said there was only one crewmember with whom they had a problem. That was someone on the atomic bomb flight over Hiroshima, the first of the two missions. The man was turned down for a regular commission and it hit him hard. He turned to a life of robbery. Olivi said, "whenever he was arrested he told the judge what he did (in the war)... and they let him go." Eventually the man died of cancer.

When we talked, Olivi expected his August 9, 1945 flight over Japan aboard a B-29 would probably be the last time he'd see the country and he didn't plan to go back. "I don't think I'd want to go around the people." He said, "we've inflicted so much damage on the people...the damage to the material things, that's nothing, but the people themselves." Olivi asked what could be said to them. "You gonna' say you're sorry? Well I'm not sorry because they started the war. He was clear it was " our duty to end the war."

Over the years there has been some debate whether it was necessary to drop an atomic bomb to end the war. Olivi agreed there are many arguments on both sides but he knew his view. "I say to some of those who feel that the bomb was unnecessary, talk to some of the Marines that were gonna' invade the Japanese Empire on November 1, 1945 and they'll give you, without equivocation, the fact that if we've got something to end the war, let's do it." He said a military invasion of Japan would have created a bloodbath with a million people killed or wounded. Olivi asked us to imagine the hue and cry from the public if there had been a way for President Truman to end the war and he didn't use it. Olivi points out an allied invasion would have had to have been fought against the entire Japanese population, "because they believed that if you died for the emperor, you'd go to heaven."

To those who argue Japan was ready to quit before the bomb was dropped, Olivi cited the fact firebombing Tokyo and dropping the first atomic bomb on Hiroshima didn't force surrender. He said it took a second bomb on Nagasaki to end the war.

Olivi didn't tire of talking about the historic mission that is now long-ago history. "I like to talk to the high school kids because we want them to know that the life we have today had to be gotten at a cost." He said, "it just wasn't handed to us. We had to do something about it. Unfortunately, somebody had to die in preserving our way of life. To me it's something to be able to tell these youngsters."

Olivi retired in 1986 from the City of Chicago where he was in charge of city bridges and its bridge tenders. If you want to see the famous Nagasaki mission B-29 that took the second atomic bomb called "Fat Man" to Japan, you can find Bockscar at the National Museum of the United States Air Force, in Dayton, Ohio. Olivi visited and climbed into the plane's co-pilot seat, but he found something had changed. "When I get in there it's a little tighter than what it used to be because I've gained weight." I told him I think those cockpits shrink. He laughingly agreed.

Getting the first of my several interviews with Olivi was a matter of going to his appearance, in this case a military collectibles show. I had arranged with the organizer to show up and he arranged for me to meet Fred. I've had to conduct interviews in a variety of settings. This one was outside the meeting hall near a dumpster. It ain't always glamorous. That interview led to a years long friendship with Fred and his appearance several times on one of my talk shows in a somewhat more comfortable setting, though there can be drawbacks in a studio too. Once I was talking with a county sheriff on the air and the station cat stepped on a control board and sent a tone out over the air. Another time the cat just pushed the mike away from my guest. But yet again I digress.

Olivi died in April, 2004, ending a life that for me will be remembered for his kindness and his clarity about the rightness of his courageous action on August 9, 1945.

At the same collectibles show where I first met Fred Olivi, I also had the chance to talk to a B-17 waist gunner. But this wasn't about just any B-17. It was the famous Memphis Belle and Bill Winchell was one of the waist gunners. At a separate occasion I interviewed Memphis Belle pilot, Robert Morgan. While the two interviews were at different places, some of their feelings were similar about the war, Hollywood and a commitment to a cause.

ROBERT MORGAN

"I'd rather be up there than down here anytime."

BILL WINCHELL

"Right straight up, he hung it on its props... the props conk out of course, then you're in a straight dive at about five thousand feet and thank heavens the props caught again. That was a little bit hairy."

Colonel Robert Morgan was a man with a mission -- actually 25 of them -- at least as far as the B-17 named Memphis Belle was concerned. Morgan piloted Memphis Belle, the famous World War II heavy bomber that was the first B-17 to finish 25 missions. That was the magic number needed to provide the crew with its ticket home in 1943. From the warfront the plane and crew moved to the homefront, touring the United States on a public relations trip. This time the mission was to thank the American people for supporting the war effort. Decades later, the Memphis Belle and the crew were made famous to a new generation of Americans with the release of the Hollywood movie. When I spoke with Morgan, he was attending the fly-in of an armada of World War II planes flying coast-to-coast to commemorate the 50th anniversary of the end of the war. Morgan saw the "Freedom Flight," as it was called, as a salute to all veterans, adding "and that's the most important thing for this Freedom Flight...not just the flying veterans, but all of them." Morgan said the event awakens some, who had, as he put it, "gone to sleep on World War II." He said young people needed to understand how the United States was truly united during the war. "It's the only time in my lifetime," he said, "that I found America 100 percent behind any one thing, and it really was. I mean civilians, veterans... military, everybody was behind the World War II effort." At the time we talked he noted "there was no dissension and we haven't had anything like that since." Some may feel that unity returned on September 11, 2001 but that was still six years in the future.

Flying was an obvious love for Morgan. "I'd rather be up there than down here anytime," he said. He found the B-17 fun to fly, a great airplane. Morgan called it the greatest formation flying airplane he flew, "and I flew 24s and I flew B-29s and it was also one airplane that would bring you back. I mean, it would take more punishment than any other airplane in World War II in the bombers."

Memphis Belle waist gunner Clarence "Bill" Winchell was quite candid when I talked with him about combat. "Anybody who ever tells you that he wasn't afraid going into combat is lying. It just scares the bejeebers out of you. You know what has to be done and you've done it before. You know what you're getting into but you go. I mean, this is your job." In those combat days Winchell and others didn't get much good news from oddsmakers. "You had about one chance in five of coming back every time you took off on a mission; one in five of coming back. So that's pretty steep odds. But we went and we went and we went. You would no more think about letting your buddies down than the man in the Moon. I mean, you don't call in sick...if they're going, it's a moral obligation...to go with 'em.

He remembers one mission when a German fighter came at them in nearly a 12 o'clock position that Winchell says was bent on ramming them. "So (pilot) Morgan whipstalled the plane." Winchell said Morgan went straight up and hung it on its props. "The props conk out of course, then you're in a straight dive at about five thousand feet and thank heavens the props caught again. That was a little bit hairy." On the same mission, the plane also got about half the tail shot out, lost an engine and had some right wing damage. "That was probably our closest we came to hittin' the silk and gettin' out of there."

Winchell wanted young people to be proud of being American and not take freedom for granted, and also to understand what people like him had to go through to allow them to be free Americans. He felt people had no concept of what aerial combat was like and believed that unless you've done it you will never know. Certainly Hollywood contributes to the misconceptions. Winchell felt strongly that the movie "Memphis Belle" is, as he put it, "not the real McCoy, by any stretch of the imagination." That was a point Robert Morgan made as well. Morgan said, "they tried to change a lot of things to cater to the young people today, the way they had the crew acting. We would have been court-martialed if we acted like that crew (in the movie) did." Bill Winchell says the most glaring error was the flight the movie B-17 took over the bombing target. In the movie, the crew is unable to see the target because of clouds, so the pilot ordered they go around and try again. Winchell said it wouldn't happen. "This is 20 minutes more where you're a sitting duck," and points out that "nobody in his right mind would do that."

Winchell says probably the best World War II flying movie was the one that became a television series, "Twelve O'Clock High." Another movie high on his list was, "Command Decision" with Clark Gable.

One famous B-29 that Robert Morgan flew was "Dauntless Dotty." In 1944 the plane, under his command, was the lead plane on the first B-29 bombing raid on Tokyo since Jimmy Doolittle led his raid with B-25s two years earlier. "Dauntless Dotty" crashed in 1945 while taking off from Kwajalein Island and the wreckage disappeared in the Pacific Ocean.

Morgan set up his own collectibles business based in Asheville, North Carolina for flight related items and died in 2004. Bill Winchell was a chemical engineer and lived in the suburbs of Chicago. He was retired when he died in 1994. As for their famous B-17, the Air Force has declared the Memphis Belle a national treasure and the plane for a time sat, appropriately, in Memphis, Tennessee, where it was dedicated on May 17, 1987, the 44th anniversary of its final mission. The National Museum of the United States Air Force later took possession of the aircraft for restoration and it went on display there in 2018.

If you find adventure on the sea to be more exciting, Lucas Brandolino and Bruno Rzona have some stories that may make you glad you're on dry land.

LUCAS BRANDOLINO

"Just hang on and that's it...Good thing the Lord held it up for 11 hours or we'd have all been down there someplace."

BRUNO RZONCA

"The bodies were piled up behind the turrets... All the body parts were laying on top of the deck...When the wave came by, the water was red of blood, so many guys."

Lucas Brandolino and Bruno Rzonca have very different backgrounds and one common link. Both men survived a ship sinking. From there the stories dramatically diverge. In 1956, Brandolino was returning from vacation in Italy aboard the famous Italian luxury liner Andrea Doria.

Lucas Brandolino and the rest of the Andrea Doria passengers and crew were about 24 hours from New York. It was July 25, 1956, nearly midnight and the fog in this part of the Atlantic was heavy that night. The icebreaker Stockholm and the luxury liner were about to become temporarily joined in the water and permanently linked in sailing history. The collision sent the Andrea Doria to the bottom, though the Stockholm, while damaged, remained afloat. Brandolino was in his 30s, single and traveling home alone. He said, "when (the Stockholm) hit the Andrea Doria, she hit her good." Before the crash but on the night of the collision, he decided he didn't want to see a movie being played on board and the ship was going to dock in port the next day, so he decided to get "a little shuteye." He went to his stateroom in the "tourist class" below the water line. "I was laying in my bunk. I wasn't actually asleep, so when it went boom I went down (on the floor). Brandolino adds, "when you start falling you're always grabbing for something...and the other guy, (his roommate) was Tony Caruso, I think it was, and he (was) a nice guy. He was from California, had beautiful black hair." Brandolino went up on deck and saw him a little later. Brandolino said Caruso's "nice black hair" had" turned all white." "He must've got a good shock, you know what I mean?"

Brandolino had his life jacket and the Andrea Doria was listing but he didn't know right away that the Andrea Doria was going to sink. "You don't know nothin'. Just hang on and that's it. Nobody knew nothin'... They didn't tell you it's gonna' sink or whatnot."

He said, "once you heard all the boom boom, whistles, whatnot, everybody knew something happened. You had different stations you were supposed to go to. We had drills on that a little bit but we all wound up on top the deck and a few of them crew people who knew what they were doin' would help you out. 'You go over here and you go over there, blah blah.'"

He said they didn't say "abandon ship" right away, "because they didn't know when it was gonna' go down anyway." He was grateful though. "Just like we say, good thing the Lord held it up for 11 hours or we'd have all been down there someplace."

Brandolino agreed with reports the Andrea Doria's crew left a lot to be desired. Okay he put it more bluntly, remembering "they were no good." He said, "they were gone, we was still there. I don't say all the crew was bad. The majority of them were. The part I seen, they were bad." Passengers seldom got any help from them, but some of the crewmembers were on top of the situation. "You get the more educated crewmen, you know, they know what's going on, they done a lot of helpin,'" but he added, "them ones that ain't too educated, they take 'em up off the street so they can have a job doing this, doing that, so them guys ain't too educated, so I guess they must've went kaput first." Brandolino said when you're on a ship, whatever your job, you get scared. "I don't know if they are told what's what, if anything happens the people go first, then the crew, or so and so, I couldn't tell ya' but I don't care, if something happens...you're always thinkin' of yourself, I think, and so that's what happened. They were gone." Brandolino was saved by the Stockholm but he said, "they took a little time, but the first ship that got there besides the Stockholm was the Ile De France and a lot of the crewmen were in them boats goin' over to the Ile De France. It wasn't our boats because our boats wouldn't go down on either side." Brandolino says that's because the ship was listing. One side is closer to the water and the other side is high. They eventually got off the ship thanks to other boats coming to the rescue. "A guy named Tony was from around New Jersey, some area, and he found a rope. We tied a rope on the women...Two or three guys hold the rope. I grabbed the women and just pushed 'em over, but there was a rope tied around 'em. The guys let the women down into the rowboats down below." The rope was unhooked, brought back up and retied around another woman. "Bingo and she went over...If you were to argue with the woman we'd have still been on the ship, ya' get it?"

When he saw the majority of the women getting off the ship, he told me, "I says 'Luke, it's about your turn' so what I did, because you grab them big ropes and if you ain't got gloves or something you get that, how would you say, they burn your hands, ya' know?" Brandolino knew how to climb down a rope. He was on the side of the Andrea Doria that was listing and closer to the water. "I went down so far, had my legs crossed. When I went down say ten, 15 feet, I stopped, took a little breather, kept going down 'til I got down there in the boat." His lifeboat was packed pretty well. Brandolino said some people always panic but what he saw "wasn't too bad...I wasn't panicking."

When we talked in 1996, Brandolino lived in Joliet and he told me his experience didn't keep him off cruise ships. "I went to Lake Michigan one time with my wife...Hell, I took a little cruise on the Lake. Well of course, you know, you're a little curious but once you get on it you get the feel you're alright."

He didn't think there was much point in bringing the Andrea Doria to the surface. "All that stuff that's been in there for years is gonna' be...all corroded and whatnot, unless they can do something with that, clean it up. I wouldn't touch it. Well I wouldn't have the money to start touching it anyway." If someone can make money on raising it, he said let them do it.

Fifty-two people died in the collision and sinking and the Andrea Doria still lies in over 200 feet of water. Brandolino seemed rather matter of fact about his experience. "If you get out of something you're alright. But if I'd have went down, goodbye, but since you survived it, hey, you feel better." He was glad it was over and said, "I survived. What more can you say?"

Bruno Rzonca also nearly lost his life at sea but in his case the British Navy was trying to kill him. As a member of the crew of the German battleship Bismarck, he too rode the Atlantic, not on vacation, but on a mission of death. The date was Tuesday, May 27, 1941. The United States was not at war, yet, but Britain was and the Bismarck was in the last day of her short life as a war machine.

After trials at sea and a visit by Adolph Hitler, battleship Bismarck left for duty. On May 24, 1941 the ship sank the British battle cruiser Hood, incurring the wrath of British Prime Minister Winston Churchill who then gave the order to sink the Bismarck. The British Navy did just that three days later.

Bruno Rzonka's job on the Bismarck included operating the catapult that launched the ship's four Arado Ar 196 seaplanes that, once in the air, returned to the ship by landing on water and being retrieved. When I talked with Rzonca in 1997 he was living in the United States. Looking back to that bloody battle that sank the ship and killed over two-thousand men, Rzonca remembers the battleship was the pride of Hitler's fleet. In his thick German accent, he told me the Bismarck had been struck with a torpedo from the air, damaging the rudder and forcing the ship to run in a circle.

The next morning the British fleet was ready for her. "In 90 minutes they shot about three thousand rounds at us. They knocked everything out. We couldn't shoot back anymore and the skipper (on the Bismarck) gave orders to sink the ship" because he was afraid "they were gonna' capture the ship." Rzonca said, "at first they give order, get ready sink the ship. You know, they open up the bottom valves in the turbine room and the boiler room and then they give order sink the ship. They blew it off so the water came in. And five minutes later I give order, 'leave the ship.'"

While the shooting was going on, Rzonca said most of those on the outside of the ship were killed but he says the men below wouldn't listen and stay put under the deck below all the shooting. "I couldn't stop them. I like to stop 'em…I say 'stay underneath' because the shooting goes out there. If you were out there they gonna' kill you." The men ran out where they were exposed to the shooting. Rzonca found an exit that was pried open so they could slide through it sideways. "When I came out it was awful, the sight. Behind the smaller turrets you know they look for cover…and the British were shooting. The bodies were piled up behind the turrets… all the body parts were laying on top of the deck. I almost stepped in one guy, you know, he had a empty stomach. You know, all the intestines were out. I don't like to talk about it."

The Bismarck was listing and Rzonca said, "when the wave came by, the water was red of blood, so many guys." The ship leaned more and more to the left or port side and Rzonca jumped, perhaps 25 feet to the water.

The ship "went down with the propeller first or what they call the stern first." The water was 50 degrees. "We had to swim for an hour before I got picked up. I was picked up by British cruiser Dorsetshire." Rzonka was lucky. One of the controversial events of the battle occurred when the British Navy says it got a warning of a German submarine in the area and the British had to get out of there. That meant leaving Bismarck survivors to die in the Atlantic. When it was over, Rzonca says the crew of 2,486 was left with 115 survivors.

It wasn't the first time Rzonca had a ship shot out from under him. Before the Bismarck he served on a cruiser during an invasion of a Norwegian harbor. "On our way out the British U-boats (as he referred to British subs) were waiting for us. One (British sub) shot three torpedoes in one time...The torpedo came in next room to me and we lost 11 sailors there." He said his ship couldn't be towed so they had to sink it themselves. With a little laugh he said, "a month later I came on the Bismarck."

After Rzonca's retrieval from the water by the British following the sinking of the Bismarck, he first was sent to a prisoner of war camp in England, then he was shipped to Canada and in 1946 was sent back to England. The next year, 1947, he returned home to Hamburg, Germany. He claimed he was treated well as a prisoner of war and later as a resident of the United States. He found Americans always friendly.

It brought up a lot of memories for Rzonca in 1989 when the remains of the Bismarck were located under the sea. "Oh yeah," he laughed, "I thought I'd get my job back." Rzonca was quick to add, "it's just a joke." Rzonka died in 2004 after surviving that close call at sea so many decades earlier.

Death at sea is a risk fisherman face too. Sebastian Junger discovered that world after the Andrea Gail went down in a "perfect storm," taking the crew with her. When I talked with him I learned his feelings about ocean storms and the fact he almost learned firsthand what it's like to drown. Now that's research.

SEBASTIAN JUNGER

"He got a bad feeling, got off the boat, and a month later he was watching the news...and it said the *Andrea Gail* was missing off...the Grand Banks and he said to his girlfriend, 'see? That was the boat I almost got on' and tragically he died a year later on another fishing boat that disappeared without a trace."

Sebastian Junger said if he were to die young, he'd want to go in dramatic fashion. In our 1997 interview he said if he were to die at an old age he would rather have his family gathered around him. The author of the true story, "The Perfect Storm" knows something about death. His bestseller, which became a top motion picture starring George Clooney, tells of the fishing boat Andrea Gail and its final, fatal journey in 1991. It's a journey that ended with boat and crew swallowed up in angry seas, never to be seen again.

Junger says the term "perfect storm" was coined by a meteorologist who believed you couldn't have designed a worse storm for the coast of New England. Junger told me a hurricane, a gale and a cold front all collided off the East Coast in a "perfectly bad way." It created 100-foot waves offshore, "and the storm retrograded, which means it went against the jetstream, which is fairly rare, and came back and hit the coast a second time," and he says that was why it was called the "perfect storm."

The Andrea Gail was a tough, 72-foot steel-hulled swordfishing boat that would go out for a month at a time. I mentioned that if anyone should be able to handle themselves in a storm it would be these guys on the Andrea Gail. Junger agreed, but added, "there's no reason to think they didn't handle themselves well. They were faced with such savage conditions that another captain said that 'had the entire swordfishing fleet of about

12 boats been right where...the Andrea Gail was, the entire fleet would have gone down.' They really were at ground zero as far as the storm was concerned." Junger says the rest of the fleet was beaten up pretty badly but they were farther to the east and didn't get the full brunt of the storm. Ship's Captain Billy Tyne and the crew of the Andrea Gail basically were "in the wrong place at the wrong time."

In a sense there actually was one survivor of the Andrea Gail and you can chalk it up to fate, God or dumb luck. A fisherman named Adam Randall hadn't worked for a while and badly needed work. His girlfriend told him he'd better get a job soon. Randall knew the boat and several members of the crew of the Andrea Gail and got so far as to be on board the day they were going to leave. "He just shook his head and he just had a bad feeling. He said he felt a cold wind." Junger said Randall felt a premonition, "and this is a guy who's fished his whole life. He wasn't a particularly queasy sort when it comes to taking risks." Randall got off the boat and "a month later he was watching the news with his girlfriend, who I guess forgave him for not taking the job, and it said the Andrea Gail was missing off... the Grand Banks and he said to his girlfriend, 'see? That was the boat I almost got on.' Tragically, he died a year later on another fishing boat that disappeared without a trace." Junger says there is a feeling among mariners there are people sort of marked for drowning and you can't avoid it. He says it's an idea that even goes back to the Greek tragedies, that fate is going to get you one way or another, and Junger says, fate got Adam Randall.

Fate nearly grabbed Sebastian Junger, too, giving him a sense of what it's like to drown. The author had surfed off Cape Cod since he was a little kid. This time it was January and he had just bought a winter wet suit. He was surfing by himself when a huge set of waves rolled through, "and the first one snapped the surfboard leash" that tied him to the surfboard, "and the next wave broke right in front of me and pinned me to the bottom. It just drove me down." He described it as "being in a huge washing machine. It just would not let go. The turbulence was so tremendous that I couldn't get back to the surface and the first wave had already kind of winded me and eventually I just started to black out. I was losing it. It's hard to tell, but it felt like I was right on the edge of blacking out, and of course, then I would have inhaled water and died. Right before I lost consciousness the wave let me go and I made it back to the beach." He'd tell you that's way too close for comfort.

Junger said the storms are "tragic but fascinating things." He researched other shipwreck and disaster at sea stories to write "The Perfect Storm" and found some of them "horrifying and compelling." For example, he spoke of the steamship Portland that "went down off Cape Cod in 1898 in a huge storm, similar to my storm actually. Four hundred people lost on that boat, I believe."

Junger starts his book, "The Perfect Storm" with a story about a fishing schooner off Gloucester that was on Georges Bank that discovered a note in a bottle. "A year earlier another fishing schooner was going down in a huge storm and someone had the time and the presence of mind to scribble on a piece of paper, a note saying goodbye to their families. You must imagine maybe 20 guys on this boat, all young, in their teens, 20s maximum. The captain might have been 24, 25 years old, and he had time to scribble a goodbye and put it in a bottle and throw it overboard."

Adventure was a longtime interest of Junger's. When the storm hit that took the Andrea Gail, Junger was working as a high climber, taking trees down. It was a job that paid a lot and really gave him a thrill. "If you ever take a tree down in a small space, say over a house, you need to have a guy up in the top of the tree with ropes and a chainsaw and that was me. It got me interested in dangerous work because I hurt myself quite badly and while I was sort of recuperating I thought 'wow,' I could write about forest firefighting, I could write about commercial fishing, all these jobs that really interested me that people didn't know that much about. He thought "'what a great thing to do,' and of course, the chapter on commercial fishing just ended up being a book in itself."

When it comes to dangerous activities Junger figured people find something exhilarating about risk and coming out of it okay. "I've worked in two different wars as a freelance correspondent, and after a close call you just never feel more alive. I think that's one element of it." Junger said as far as the fisherman are concerned they aren't in the business for the thrill. "They're in it because it's really the only way they can make fairly good money. You know, they're not gonna' be lawyers and doctors, realistically." As he told me in our 1997 interview, "Gloucester's a pretty bankrupt town, and it's a tough town. These guys are fishing 'cause they have to and 'cause they've been fishing out of Gloucester for 400 years and it's just what people do there."

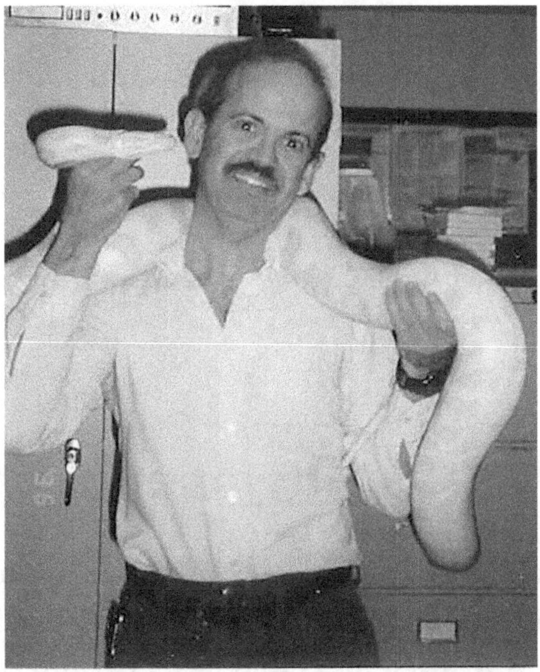

Not all of my guests on the talk shows I've hosted had two legs. This is Sunshine, an Albino Python at WKBM in Wilmington

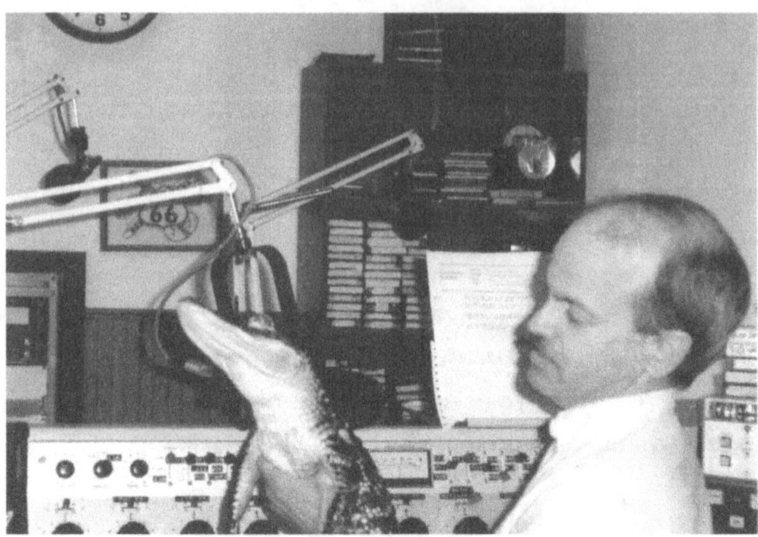

Another live guest on my WKBM talk show. When an alligator talks, it's best to listen.

In this book, we've talked about death; we've discussed taxes. How about some sex? That wasn't an offer. It was a clever way of leading into an interview with a woman whose writings lead us into sex. Erica Jong had a new book to pitch but she was well aware of the impact an earlier book of hers had, called, "Fear of Flying."

ERICA JONG

"I think the sexual revolution is much overrated. I think that we're still teaching our children that sex equals death and that if you're a bad girl or boy you'll drop dead."

The fear of flying took on a whole new meaning, thanks to author Erica Jong. Her novel by that name became a part of the American culture and she said in our 1997 interview the influence of "Fear of Flying" continued to that day. Jong said younger readers were discovering the book. "I see them in bookstores and sometimes they've been turned on by friends, sometimes they've read "Fear of Flying" in an American literature course in college. I don't think that "Fear of Flying" needs that much explanation to them." She says it is a "novel of growing up, a novel of a young woman trying to find out who she is, breaking away from her family and trying to assert her own identity." Jong said, "as such, a lot of people read it and are very moved by it -- a lot of young women and young men." She said the sexuality was stressed when the book first came out and seen as a particularly sexy book, and later was seen as a novel of growing up. She called that very important and noted "Fear of Flying" "had taken its place alongside the "Catcher in the Rye" and books like that as an American novel of growing up.

Interested in writing? Put up the yellow caution tape. Writers face a difficult profession that Jong said at the time may have been getting worse. She told me in our 1997 interview that "writers are really in a tough situation. There are so many other genres competing for our attention, but I think nothing transmits the kind of depth and the kind of inspiration that a book transmits." She said, "the relationship between a book and a reader is very intimate and that's not so with television. I think that people can take books to bed with them, they can take books to quiet places to sit and read. They read in the bathroom, they read in the kitchen, and there's a great intimacy between the book and the person reading it. It's almost as if the barrier between the two of them disappears and they become one."

We might have been more of a "sound bite" culture but that didn't change the way Jong wrote. She said then and it's probably still true the sound bite mentality does apply to promoting the book and describing it in 20 words or less. But she said maybe because there were so many sound bites around us, people were "more interested in things that go deep." She added, "intellectual fast food, you know, goes very fast but it doesn't leave you with much." People would come to her at bookstores with books they've read and loved that they've underlined and dog-eared. She said when we spoke she had "been a part of their conversation for 25 years and that's very inspiring to me as a writer."

Jong said the sexual revolution was "much overrated." Did we win? She didn't know. "It's true that there's more openness in speech, more openness in media," but Jong added at the time, " I think that we're still teaching our children that sex equals death and that if you're a bad girl or boy you'll drop dead. I don't think that we've made that much progress in dealing with sexuality in our lives. I'm sorry to have to say this." Jong felt in '97 the pendulum was perhaps swinging back in a Victorian manner. "There is a lot of backlash going on."

Jong set out to tell the tale of history from a woman's point of view, "and it's always been part of my inspiration to fill in the blanks, write the missing books." In her book, "Inventing Memory," Jong wrote about the Jewish family. She loved the Yiddish proverb that was used a lot in her family. The saying is "you can't dance at two weddings with one behind." She found Yiddish proverbs have "great humor and a kind of tragic side as well." Another one she quoted is "when a rogue kisses you, count your teeth."

On the subject of marriage, Jong, who in 1997 was eight years into her fourth marriage, says it's easier to be married when you're older. "You appreciate the other person and there's less of this restless feeling that somewhere the grass is greener, because you've been through enough to know all the problems you can have in life."

Sometimes one event or catchphrase can be forever linked to a person. The phrase that she said would be on her tombstone is the "Zipless Encounter," to use a softer word. She added, "I can't bear it but there it is." Incidentally, the "Zipless," uh, "Encounter" is defined by Jong as a perfect sexual fantasy perhaps at an elevator or an intersection. Encounter is a euphemism for a stronger word that if I were to put it in this book, I might be responsible for an encounter with a paramedic for you if you're a sensitive type. Jong said it was a phrase that had really caught on and had "become part of the language and influenced people's sexuality, influenced their sexual fantasies and there it is and I'm stuck with it."

Jong believed she'd developed a body of work with many books that have moved people and she was very grateful. But for a new writer she said it was very hard. It wasn't good news when she said at the time, "publishers are not looking for new writers. They're looking for really established commodities where they feel they can make their money back, and really it's too bad because publishing is not the kind of business where you can predict. Taste changes very quickly. The writers who were big in the past may not be big tomorrow. I think publishers have made a big mistake in throwing away tremendous millions on ghost-written celebrity books where the majority of money has gone." Jong added in '97, "sometimes these books work, but very often they don't and the publisher is left holding the bag with a huge advance." As an example, she named former O.J. Simpson prosecutor Marcia Clark who, Jong said, got a nearly five million dollar advance for her book. Unfortunately for Clark, the book didn't "earn out" and the copies were coming back, as Jong said, "by the truckload." She wanted publishers to nurture those relationships between authors and readers that go on for years. Jong said sometimes by the time a book appears, the celebrity is no longer on television and the publisher is stuck. But if you're a new writer, her advice was to never give up. "The way that you know that you're really a writer is that you're very tenacious." She said in our 1997 interview it wasn't impossible to get a first book published. Just know that "most publishers don't read unsolicited manuscripts and that your first job is to find an agent." Use the resources and write to the agent and send a small writing sample. Ask the agent if they want to represent you. She added, "despite how tough it is, people are looking for new writers." Of course that perspective was offered a while back but it came from an established writer and I can only imagine the situation hasn't improved for new writers, but write on, okay? Right on! (as long as we're pulling up old expressions.)

From sex and zipless "encounters" we can take a 180-degree shift to virtue and sweetness and everything wholesome. Zuzu and her petals, Christmas and Jimmy Stewart, savings and loan disasters...Okay so not everything about the movie "It's a Wonderful Life" was wonderful, but it did have a little girl who turned out to be a wonderful example of the movie's ideals. I caught up with (there I go again with that expression) a busy Karolyn Grimes by telephone.

KAROLYN GRIMES

"Look daddy. Teacher says every time a bell rings, an angel gets his wings."

When Karolyn Grimes was only six years old she was not only acting alongside Jimmy Stewart and Donna Reed. Grimes was held in Stewart's arms onscreen in the classic 1947 film, "It's a Wonderful Life," and it was Grimes who spoke perhaps the most famous line in one of the most famous movies. When the Bailey family's troubles reached a happy conclusion, everyone gathered around the Christmas tree. A bell rang and Grimes, as the character Zuzu, spoke the words, "every time a bell rings, an angel gets his wings." It wasn't her first movie and it wouldn't be her last. She would also play the daughter of David Niven and Loretta Young and the young friend of Cary Grant in "The Bishop's Wife," later remade into "The Preacher's Wife" with Denzel Washington and was in many more movies. But it's the film "It's a Wonderful Life" that helped guide her life. Grimes said we see the character of George Bailey, played by Jimmy Stewart, and we see someone we'd model ourselves after. As an example Grimes pointed to the moment in the film when the town tyrant, Henry Potter, offers George a job for $20,000 a year for three years. When we talked in 1997 she said the job would be hard to turn down. "Of course it would be different money but I mean, that would have been easy street for him and he could have had it made, but he knew when he shook (Potter's) hand it wasn't the right thing to do, so he had values."

Grimes said most of us have thought, at one time or another, that our dreams have not been fulfilled, and she said maybe the movie gives people a chance to reflect and makes them feel better and more in tune with their own lives. She said the movie also connects with people on the subject of friends. "Every little thing you do touches another life." She was asked by a middle school teacher in Texas to do an interview with one of his students. Despite her busy schedule she did a phone interview. Later she found he had won first place for the state of Texas. "If I had not done the interview it probably wouldn't have happened, but because I did, it touched his life." She added, "for ten minutes of mine, he got a really neat prize and maybe even some part of his future started."

Grimes' films gave her some high caliber "home movies" too. There aren't too many people from that era with such quality film footage of themselves at age six. She did 16 movies and she had copies of most of them. "It's just kind of a neat thing to do, to watch as I grew up over the years and how I changed, and to compare myself with my grandchildren and my children...pretty cool!"

Grimes didn't regret being so young when she knew some of Hollywood's legends of the 1940s. I would have thought she would have wanted to relate to them more as an adult. But Grimes said if she had been older "I probably wouldn't have acted naturally and as it was, I just thought they were just like my next door neighbor. They were nothing different or special. Thank God my mother, I guess, instilled in me that they were just like you and me, you know? I didn't know any different that they were movie legends. 'Course, you must realize, at the time they weren't the movie legends that they are today." Grimes says they were box office successes. but not at the level we later placed them.

"It's a Wonderful Life" might be called her signature movie but Grimes laughed, saying "for six minutes of film footage I have fame." She was also right when she said it's pretty cool.

Her memories of Jimmy Stewart were of someone very patient and gentle. "Kids screw up and have to do lines over and stuff," but she said he was very kind about it. Grimes said this was Stewart's first movie after the war and at this point in his life he had never married. "So he was very good with us kids, really and truly, considering the fact that, you know, he'd never had any children."

In the final scene of the movie it looks like she's hanging onto his neck for dear life. "I am indeed," she said. Was she afraid she'd fall? "Well, you know, he's very tall!" Stewart was six foot four and Grimes added, "I mean, if you're a little kid and if you're hanging on up there, that's pretty tall! You're pretty well up there. So I was hanging on like a little frog on his back when he was coming down the stairs and he was just really kind and gentle, and it must have been pretty tough because he had one kid under his arm and me on his back, so that would have been pretty good."

Moviemaking can be odd in at least one respect. Okay, probably in several respects but the one I'm talking about is the fact Grimes spent the entire movie with Jimmy Stewart, but her memories of Stewart's co-star, Donna Reed were, well, non-existent. "I was never in a scene with Donna Reed."

They were standing together next to the Christmas tree at the end of the movie, but "I never had any interaction with her at all. I don't even remember Donna Reed." That's understandable for a child of six.

Her character of Zuzu originally had an expanded role. There were three scripts that director Frank Capra bought. One of them had Zuzu very ill and going to heaven to get her deceased grandfather to help her dad who was in terrible trouble. But that version of the beginning of the story was never filmed. Grimes said, "Capra took those three stories and put them together and made his own version."

As a child she was not asked for her input into the story. "They tell you exactly what to do. You're like a little puppet," said Grimes. She laughed and said you have an on-and-off switch, "and you're on-and-you're off." She said you're well disciplined and do what you're told to do, "otherwise you wouldn't be there."

Grimes remembers Frank Capra was thrilled to see his film become the great success it did, but he also lived long enough to feel that they had butchered his favorite film because of the colorization process. That's the technique where color is artificially added to a black and white film.

She agreed television had done a lot for some of the old movies. She noted "It's a Wonderful Life" got its exposure, because "it became public domain and all the little TV stations around the United States could show it and it was free. See, somebody forgot to renew the contract in the early '70s and that's how it happened. So then it was shown everywhere and everybody really got the chance to see the movie and that's when it really became a success."

Grimes' career at such a young age included the films "Rio Grande" with John Wayne, "Blue Skies" with Bing Crosby, "Pardon My Past" with Fred MacMurray and "Hans Christian Anderson" with Danny Kaye. But before she was a teen her mother got ill, and when Grimes was 14, her mother died. When she was 15 her father was killed in an automobile crash. That was the end of her days in Hollywood. When she attended L. A. High School there were 900 kids in her class, but that world was about to change. Grimes was now an orphan and the court sent her back to live in a Missouri town where the entire population was only 800. "So that was culture shock," said Grimes. But after a year and a half she decided she loved Midwestern people. "I had never been exposed to people that had liked me for myself and I had really true friends and people that really cared about me. It was a whole different world for me." She told me in '97 "I decided I'd never go back to the Hollywood scene again and so I have not done that." She didn't regret not continuing acting and, in fact, surprised me with a comment I don't think you hear very often from an actor. Said Grimes, "quite frankly, I don't think I was that talented." She didn't think she would have done very well, "and a lot of my friends, you know, got into drugs and different things."

Rejection as a teenager is, as she put it, "really, really tough to overcome and that's what happens, because your bodies change and you get too old or too young for parts." Grimes believed there's that time when you're told you're not needed as an actor and that's tough because a teenager is already vulnerable. She said you tend to take the wrong path unless you have good parenting. "I'm very lucky that there was an angel on my shoulder that took me out of that scene and I didn't have to make those kinds of choices."

Grimes was in a rare position to see the problems of the young TV stars who have trouble and she absolutely understood their situation. She said when the industry is through with someone, "they are through with you. They don't even know your name." Worse than that, said Grimes, is the action by some parents who exploit their children.

One of Grimes' books is "Zuzu Bailey's It's a Wonderful Life Cookbook" that includes recipes from other cast members from the film. It has great titles for the recipes including "Potter the Crab Cakes" and "Frank's Creamed Capra Corn." One recipe was exchanged on the set when they made the movie, a recipe that belonged to Beulah Bondi who played Jimmy Stewart's mother in not just one, but six movies.

Despite her positive experience on "It's a Wonderful Life" the movie wasn't Karolyn Grimes' favorite to work on. "I kind of have to think that there were two others that I really liked better." She enjoyed "Rio Grande" with John Wayne because the cast and crew were on location in Moab, Utah, for three weeks. That was a lot of fun for her, "and I got to do a lot of strange things there, you know, like riding covered wagons with Indians chasin' you and stuff like that." She said, "It's a Wonderful Life" was just a regular job. There wasn't anything particularly great except for the snow. Having grown up in Hollywood, it was her first experience seeing even a simulation of snow.

Her favorite movie to work on was "The Bishop's Wife" which came out the next year, 1948, where she played the daughter of David Niven and Loretta Young. There was a good reason or rather person to make it her favorite; Cary Grant. "He was just (her voice drops to a whisper) magnificent." She said, "he played with me every day and it was just fabulous and I loved that very much." Cary Grant used to pull her around on a sled and "he'd come get me every day at lunch, by golly, and he really did ice skate and he would pull me around on this ice skating rink that we had there. He loved to tell me stories. He just loved kids, and you know, children can sense that." She knew he was sincere and "he'd search me out. He'd just have a blast."

Grimes recalled the climate of that set was not as stress free as "It's a Wonderful Life." On the "Wonderful Life" movie set everyone got along very well, but on "The Bishop's Wife" there was a little more complication and stress, and she figured Cary Grant might have been turning away from that problem by having fun with her.

"The Bishop's Wife" was remade into "The Preacher's Wife" and while Grimes had not yet seen the movie when we talked, she said she generally didn't like remakes of the old movies. "I don't think they can ever recapture what the old film had to say. Not very often do I like a sequel. They're usually not as good as the original."

The topic of movie residuals came up and got the biggest laugh of our interview. "Not hardly!" She says, "I wouldn't be schlepping cookbooks," as she continued to laugh. Good point.

She lost her husband to cancer two years before we talked, but Karolyn Grimes still described her life as wonderful. "With time, everything gets better and I have such a wonderful life now thank you to "It's a Wonderful Life." Grimes considered it a wonderful balance. "I think I had to go through a lot of tragedies in my life to get to the path I'm on now because I touch so many lives because of this movie. So many people have entered into my life and I travel all over the United States. People share their stories with me about how the movie has affected their lives." Grimes called it a responsibility she thought she'd been honed for, for some reason, and felt she'd learned to have compassion and empathy for people. She said a lot of people have changed their minds about suicide after seeing the movie. Grimes had people come up to her and share their stories of how the movie gave them hope when they were at low points in their lives. One story she shared with me was about a woman who was a radio DJ who interviewed her and after the interview the DJ told Grimes about her brother who was killed when his Air Force plane went down. "It's a Wonderful Life" was the woman's brother's favorite movie. After the man was killed the sister picked up a bell and rang it. Grimes found that very poignant, "because I know she felt like she was doing something. You can't do anything but she felt like she was at least doing that much."

There's a scene in the movie where Donna Reed, as Mary, whispers in George Bailey's deaf ear that she will love him until the day she dies. Grimes said, "I've had people that have engraved their rings. One says, 'so and so, I will love you,' and the other ring says, 'so and so, 'til the day I die.'"

The movie has made a lasting impression on many people and certainly Karolyn Grimes became a wonderful ambassador of the positive spirit of "It's a Wonderful Life." That passion even moved to the Internet with a website zuzu.net to share stories and give people a greater chance to connect with the movie.

My guess is you either respected or distrusted Johnnie Cochran Jr. The lead lawyer for the O.J. Simpson criminal double murder trial unleashed some strong feelings in the American public during the trial. All of that hoopla created an image in my mind too. But that mental picture didn't match when I sat down with him backstage at Chicago's DuSable Museum's auditorium on the city's south side.

JOHNNIE COCHRAN JR.

There are a lot of things that I had, that I've handled, that are more important to me, but at the same time I suppose that Simpson and I will be forever intertwined."

Johnnie Cochran surprised me. He was not what I expected. The image I had gathered from all of the media coverage of him seemed to paint a picture more like the slick, fast-talking lawyer, Jackie, on the TV show "Seinfeld." But the famed attorney was more soft spoken with a more thoughtful demeanor than at least I would have expected. Cochran successfully defended O.J. Simpson against the criminal charges of murdering his wife Nicole and her friend Ron Goldman. Cochran told me the year and a half on the case was a time in his life that he could not have foreseen, "an interesting period of time." But when I spoke with Cochran he didn't consider the Simpson case to be the highlight of his career. He expected the connection with O.J. Simpson would probably be with him for the rest of Cochran's life and he supposed that was okay. But he added, "I'd like to be remembered for more than that. I mean, there were a number of things that I was involved in that I consider, you know, certainly more important."

He included in his career the case of the former Black Panther Geronimo Pratt. At the time of our 1997 interview he was still working to get Pratt freed after nearly 30 years in prison for the Santa Monica, California murder of a woman. Four months after our interview Pratt was freed when his conviction was vacated. The judge ruled Pratt had not been given a fair trial and said prosecutors withheld evidence. Pratt had maintained his innocence. Cochran also said many of his civil cases he handled in Los Angeles have "left a lasting imprint on the community." He included among them, the elimination of the police "choke hold" grip used against suspects. "So," says Cochran, "there are a lot of things that I had, that I've handled that are more important to me, but at the same time I suppose that Simpson and I will be forever intertwined from the standpoint of handling that case."

Cochran agreed high profile cases tend to put people in boxes, "much more than you'd rather." When we talked he said he thought of himself as basically a trial lawyer, a litigator who did mostly civil litigation. But he said he may always be remembered as a criminal lawyer. "I'm that also, but not primarily," said Cochran at the time.

During the Simpson trial, at one of the defense meetings, fellow Simpson attorney Robert Shapiro asked how many people in the room thought Simpson was guilty. Cochran said, "none of us raised our hands. We thought that was a very strange question because Simpson always, always maintained his innocence." He added, "every lawyer who's ever handled the case would say the same thing." Cochran expected Simpson's reaction and said, "it was always very consistent." He also said "everything he ever told us always checked out."

As the criminal trial verdict was about to be announced by the jury, Cochran looked at juror number six when he came out. He said that's the first time he knew (the defense) would win. "He looked at me and looked back in a way that I told Mr. Simpson he's going home." Cochran said Simpson didn't say much at that time, just thank you. "He's always been very, very thoughtful about that." Cochran quoted Simpson as saying "thank you for saving my life."

Though found not guilty in the criminal trial, Simpson was found legally and financially liable in a civil trial. Cochran wasn't the defense attorney in that case. He called the civil trial "O.J. light." Cochran said he felt that it was important for the verdict to have credibility that the jury have "some diversity, number one." And secondly, that the jury must have "a chance to hear the evidence, I mean whatever it was, on both sides." He also wanted an appellate court to review some of the rulings. "If your defense is that I didn't do this, I didn't commit these crimes and that I possibly was framed or they said there was planting of evidence and that one of the primary people you think is involved in that may be a detective and you're not even allowed to call him, it's very tough, very tough," said Cochran. He also questioned other rulings in the civil case that he said were probably contrary to the state of the law. His objections included the makeup of the civil jury that Cochran said was weighted with people who thought Simpson was guilty.

Cochran liked and respected most of the members of the criminal defense team, but he didn't like the term "Dream Team." Cochran said they "were just lawyers trying to do a job," and added the lawyers "stood strong" and understood "it's not a popularity contest. It's to do the best you can, ethically and morally."

Cochran says the glove demonstration was critical to the criminal defense case. As you might remember from the trial, Simpson stood before the jury and tried on the glove that supposedly belonged to the killer and purportedly had been discovered by police. Simpson held it up, showing how it stretched over his hand and appeared not to fit. "We felt, from that point on, clearly we had a good chance of winning the case." Whether the glove actually fit or why it didn't is a matter for you to debate, but Cochran saw it as an important moment in the trial. Perhaps just as memorable in the trial was Cochran's line in his summation to the jury where he told them, referring to the glove, "if it doesn't fit, you must acquit."

Cochran said expert witness for the defense, Doctor Henry Lee's statement that something was wrong with the prosecution's case, was also really important for the defense. He called Lee a "magnificent witness."

In our interview Cochran said he was saddened by the polarization of society after the Simpson case. "The racial gaps, racial divide that Simpson revealed were there all along," he said. Cochran added, "if you're part of the majority community, it's very easy to overlook that and not have to address it because nobody wants to talk about race in this country," Cochran said W.E.B. Dubois, in his seminal work, "The Souls of Black Folk," in 1903, said the problem of the color line would be the problem of the 20th century. Cochran believed he was right, adding "it's going to be the problem of the 21st century, unless we have some moral leadership in this country, and somebody takes the bull by the horns and addresses this question, and we start talking about how we see things differently, based on our life experiences." Cochran said, "it wasn't created by Simpson. It just gave us an opportunity now, however... to address the issues and try to move forward together in the new millennium and I think that's one of the things that we're missing out on if we don't do it....I feel real strongly about that." Cochran died in 2005, probably forever professionally linked to O.J. Simpon.

"Know Your Constituents" Will County Coroner Pat O'Neil or at least his campaign seemed to understand product placement.

SIGN HERE, SO I CAN SAY I WAS HERE

WHEN YOU'RE INTERVIEWING a notable type, you figure you should be above the crass act of asking for an autograph. Asking for one also removes some of the objectivity you've placed between yourself and the celebrity. At times, when your ego is flying at full staff, you think they should be asking for your autograph. But then you also realize you can't pass up a chance to get one for the collection. Sure, I have their voice recorded talking to me and that's certainly a form of autograph. In fact at one time it was becoming a popular way of autograph hunting. Seekers of the "Sacred Scribble" were sticking a tape recorder in the face of their favorite celebrity. But it still lacks something.

I've collected some good signatures while on the job from people such as Jan Berry from Jan and Dean and Johnnie Cochran Jr. But I've missed out on some that I now will never get, such as Art Scholl, the stunt pilot killed while filming "Top Gun."

At least in a few cases I did have the foresight to take photos or ask someone to take them. As I've posted in this book I photographed Art Scholl, with his dog, Aileron, on his shoulder. While I never interviewed Juwan Howard, I also took some pictures of the standout basketball player at the 1990 Morris, Illinois Coca Cola Shootout, and darned if Howard didn't go on to big time B-Ball and big money.

Future NBA player Juwan Howard shows his reach at the high school Coca Cola Shoootout in Morris, Illinois, in 1990. I wish I'd been better at sports photography then

By now you must know I like to meet and greet notable types. But only the elite. The pica types don't interest me. That's a little typewriter humor there. I wish I had my recorder with me the time I went to a Dizzy Gillespie jazz concert at the Rialto Square Theater in Joliet. The tickets were courtesy of the radio station, a small perk, but you take what you can. After the concert, a friend and I, the same one who once said during a parade, while I carried my camera, "Biff, there's the mayor, shoot him," went to the stage door parking lot. You'd think I would have learned to be careful when Chris and I were with celebrities. I could imagine Chris saying, "Biff, there's the trumpet player, make him dizzy."

Anyway, after the show, outside the Rialto, there were four of us waiting. One young guy had a horn with him. Dizzy not only took time to talk with us and seemed in no hurry, he actually wanted to hear the kid play. Geez, no pressure there for him huh? What does it normally take to get a nearly private audition with Dizzy Gillespie? Even if it is in a parking lot, late at night. The kid did play two or three notes. Dizzy's reaction? He told the guy to keep practicing. I don't remember the context of that, but either way I suppose it's encouragement from a jazz great.

Dizzy told me about someone he used to know named Biff. Then I asked him if playing were as much fun as it used to be. He looked around and actually said, "it's a pain in the ass." I loved that. I asked him to write that on the show flyer I carried. He wrote, To Biff, P I T A. Actually, it looks like P T T A. So he stammered a bit. I still treasure that flyer.

By now you also know I love history and historic figures, particularly those who will talk to me. As you learned with Egyptian President Anwar Sadat assasination shooting victim Jerald Agenbroad, just because you aren't a famous name doesn't mean you can't play some role in shaping or witnessing history. Madeleine Brown falls into both categories. You probably don't know her name, but you know about the father of her son. You don't know her face but you'll be interested in knowing what she knew about the Kennedy assassination. You don't know...oh what the heck, why not get to know her as I did with a phone call to Texas?

MADELEINE BROWN

"Lyndon screamed in my ear that after tomorrow, being November the 22, the Kennedys...would never embarrass him again."

If you're going to have an affair, you may as well pick somebody with a future. Madeleine Brown of Dallas, Texas, did just that when she started her affair with a congressman. That, by itself, wouldn't be much of a story. But this congressman had just been elected to the U.S. Senate and would one day become the 36th President of the United States. Lyndon Johnson's career was on the rise and Madeleine Brown was right there along the way. Brown also said her affair with LBJ produced a son, Steven Mark Brown.

As an advertising executive in the city of Dallas, Brown knew some other high and low level people, including billionaire H.L. Hunt and Jack Ruby, the killer of Lee Harvey Oswald. Brown's story takes an even stranger twist when she reveals what LBJ said to her the day before President John Kennedy was assassinated.

When she first met Lyndon Johnson at a party at the Adolphus Hotel in Dallas there was a chemistry between them. In the fall of 1948 she said he put a key in her hand and she went to his apartment to begin what she called a "wonderful, loving affair." Brown's book, "Texas in the Morning," paints a picture of a passionate Lyndon Johnson, with Brown seeing a side she said probably no one else saw. "He was a loving, passionate person with me." She also wrote about his temper and told me, "oh, I think the public really knew that he was really high strung, high tempered, but I only saw that side of him when I became pregnant with Steven and then when I asked him about the (JFK) assassination." Brown's book doesn't portray a pretty picture of Texas politics. She said "they controlled Washington. It was power and more power -- money, power, oil -- it had controlled Washington since 1901 when they found the big gusher here in Texas."

On a personal level, Brown found Lyndon Johnson "tall and strong and possibly presented a father image to me. He was so strong and his appearance demanded respect." Brown got an idea that Johnson's wheeling and dealing was not always on the up and up after the "Stuffed Box 13" election scandal. The "Stuffed Box 13" scandal was the 1948 election that won a Senate seat for LBJ and brought J. Edgar Hoover to Texas to investigate. After that she said she "knew then that he was powerful and he could wheel and deal." Brown said people stuck together and nothing was done about the election scandal. When Johnson was criticized that he was doing some shady stuff, Brown said he would laugh and say, "I'm a country boy. I get the job done." She quoted him saying, "while people are standing around scratchin'and pickin' their nose...ol' Lyndon's out there and I get the job done."

Another figure, well known in downtown Dallas and eventually worldwide, was Jack Ruby. Brown knew him too, personally. In 1963, Ruby, of course, would go down in history as the man who shot and killed Lee Harvey Oswald, the purported assassin of President Kennedy. Ruby ran the Carousel Club, a strip club in Dallas. If Jack Ruby saw you on the street, Brown said, "he'd jump out in front of ya' and he'd say, 'I'm Jack Ruby, I want you to come down to the Carousel Club' and he'd call everyone 'classy.'" Brown said, "he was a real strange person but I liked ol' Jack." She said he ran with the power people in Dallas and "he knew everything that was going on here." But she found Jack Ruby likeable. "Oh yes, yes," she said, "and he had the most beautiful brown eyes you ever saw. They were like raw diamonds, I guess. They'd sparkle when he'd grin." Her acquaintance with him, however, never gave her an indication of his murderous inclinations, but she said, "we knew he was the gangster of the mob and we just didn't cross over the lines. Dallas didn't have organization in those days and everybody sort of minded their own business." Brown recalled, "if you wanted to be a prostitute, you'd go down and get a health card...and the police knew who you were." She said, "if you wanted to gamble, Jack Ruby knew where to go. They had contracts on people. If you wanted to have someone whipped, you'd pay 'em ten dollars." Brown said if you wanted them killed, shell out maybe a hundred. If you wanted an abortion, you could go to a clinic where they would charge 25 dollars, no names asked. There just simply wasn't any real organization in Dallas. She added the city had been called a murder capital of the world almost from the time it was established.

Of course, one murder in the city changed world history. On November 21, 1963, the day before John Kennedy was assassinated, Brown said some power brokers had a meeting in Dallas. They had a social where she was invited. The party was sort of breaking up, "and all these people went into a conference and when they came out, Lyndon screamed in my ear that after tomorrow, being November the 22, the Kennedys – and of course he never referred to them with nice names, they were terrible names -- he said they would never embarrass him again." On the morning of the assassination, Lyndon called her. "It was the Texas Hotel and he repeated the same message that they were never going to embarrass him again," Brown thought then he was just angry, but she had second thoughts after the assassination. After Johnson told her the oil people and intelligence were involved in the assassination, she said, "my body went to hyperventilating." She said people in Dallas immediately began saying LBJ was involved, but she didn't want to hear such things.

Brown said LBJ admitted to her that he knew the assassination was coming, but he didn't do anything to stop it. Could he have stopped it? "I doubt it because the oil people were so irate and angry and of course, by then, the intelligence was in it, and it was over John Kennedy and the oil depletion and these oil people were being hurt. They were being put out of business…Their income was cut 25 percent. It was the oil people and their intermingling of the power that caused all of this."

Knowing what she knew didn't stop her love for Johnson. "If you love someone, you love 'em. You don't turn it on or off. You certainly aren't pleased with their actions, but as far as a heartfelt feeling -- that does not change, in my opinion." She called her relationship with Lyndon "very much of a marriage, just the other family that's all." When we talked she said, after all of the years, and even though he was long dead, she still found him exciting.

Brown had the chance to meet Lady Bird Johnson and her daughters and said Lady Bird and the girls didn't have any inclination of what was going on. "The only thing Lady Bird has ever said – she's never confirmed or denied -- she said that Lyndon loved women and half the population is women but (Lady Bird) knew one thing -- he liked her the best."

The last time Madeleine Brown met with Lyndon Johnson was August 1969 when she was invited to an event in Houston with lunar astronauts. She had hoped Johnson would publicly acknowledge Steven Brown as his son. She said LBJ accepted him and though Lyndon provided financial support, he never publicly acknowledged the son who died in 1990.

Brown considered herself a part of history. "It's just one of the things that happens to people in their lives," she said. "I've never had any adverse publicity or anything." Incidentally, she had also had not slept in the White House Lincoln Bedroom. Maybe that takes a political contribution.

But then if you're looking for a place to stay, it isn't up to Lincoln Bedroom standards, but writer and Motel 6 pitchman Tom Bodett had some opinion on that. He, too, was promoting a book when I met him in the Chicago area. It was time to see how he felt about his perhaps permanent connection with a memorable catchphrase.

TOM BODETT

"It'll probably be chiseled on my gravestone and I've left in my will that if that happens I'm going to come back and haunt those people and their descendants."

Tom Bodett will probably always be associated with that well-known catchphrase for Motel 6. You know the saying the chain adapted to its needs about how it will "leave the light on for ya'." When we talked, Bodett joked that he had no doubt it would be his eulogy. "It'll probably be chiseled on my gravestone and I've left in my will that if that happens I'm going to come back and haunt those people and their descendants." He laughed, pointing out "I'm kidding." But when we talked in 1996 the saying was everywhere he went. "It's something...like a singer who has a hit song who is continually asked to sing it. That's what it is, and although it probably doesn't have the excitement around it that it might have ten years ago, it is the thing that people very much know me for, and it's maybe one of the things that attracts people to my other work, so I'd be an idiot to feel badly about the fact that they know me at all."

His other work is extensive. Bodett wrote fiction and non-fiction, appeared on National Public Radio and hosted a television travel series called "America's Historic Trails," a combination history and travel show telling about America's sights and sites.

With work in both print and broadcast, which was more freeing for him? "Same thing to me. To do it, it's identical because literally all of my printed work started as radio work and then was adapted for print." (Actually that's the case with much of this book you're reading.) Bodett told me what he enjoyed about the medium of radio was its "real intimate setting." He said as people listen, "probably they're alone, listening to everything we're saying." He described it as spending "one to one time" with people on the radio and said, "that's why I really like the medium. You can be very personal and very intimate in that way. What I like about print is that it's permanent. Somebody can read a book and read it again or they can give it to a friend if they like something, or they can read part of it to a friend that they like, which is something you can't do in radio. Radio just kind of goes right by you. It's sort of in the moment and then it's gone and so I like both mediums. I couldn't imagine being in just one of them. It would drive me crazy."

Bodett figured the fact he was a neophyte, a novice in broadcasting, made him attractive to the Motel 6 chain. "I'd only been in broadcast a couple of years and living in Homer, Alaska. I'd never had any kind of voice coaching or anything else. I was just delivering like I talk." They liked the fact he didn't sound like everybody else on the radio. "I didn't have one of those over modulated kind of, you know, (in a "radio" voice) 'welcome, this is WKKK,' you know, just one of those announcer voices." He said they found that attractive.

In 1996 when we talked he was living in Homer (again speaking in a deeper "radio" tone) "so I don't pick up that voice." He agreed his special appeal worked for him with National Public Radio, too. "Yeah, they like it for the same reason and NPR makes a great effort to find new voices out around the country and not just, you know, those broadcasters in

New York and L. A. who are on the fast track. They have a long history of introducing new people to the country."

I asked if he were flattered or irritated when people compared him to radio storyteller Garrison Keillor. "I'm sure those comparisons annoy him more than they do me. No, I don't find it in the least bit annoying. The similarities are all valid. I mean we're both a couple of deep voice guys who grew up in the Midwest and like people in small towns." However, Bodett said they had two very different takes on the world. "Both of us can be enjoyed separately or not."

Before our interview, Bodett gave a reading of his book to a bookstore audience. Afterwards, Bodett told me he thought someone in the audience had asked if Bodett and Keillor had considered doing a storytelling jam session. Bodett didn't take to that idea. "Doesn't that sound awful?" He laughed when he said, "that was a very funny idea though."

Proving his "we'll leave the light on for you" phrase definitely is a part of his life, I had to ask him to do, what is called in radio, a "liner." It's just a phrase from the interviewee promoting the person or radio station. But as I found in the case of a similar request of actor John Astin, there is a problem with asking someone to use a famous phrase in a commercial application outside the original use. I wanted him to say, "sometimes Biff Jannuzzi may seem to be in the dark, but don't worry. I'm Tom Bodett and we'll leave the light on for you." The problem, as he explained, was that he didn't own the Motel 6 phrase. He told me he'd be glad to give me a liner but Motel 6 asked that he not use its trademark to promote other things. But he found a way to get around the restriction. The liner came out as "sometimes Biff Jannuzzi may seem to be in the dark, but don't worry. I'm Tom Bodett and we'll, well, you know." When you think about it, that may be even better.

Maybe travel isn't your thing. Maybe you hate long drives and living in a motel room out of a suitcase. Maybe Margie McCauley has the answer. She traveled across country but she didn't always stay in a motel. No big deal you say? Okay, how about this? Margie McCauley traveled from California to Chicago and she did it on foot!

MARGIE MCCAULEY

"I have driven through there and I'd always say, 'well why can't I get out of this terrible place?' and walking through there, it was like being in space…and you just look over and see the freeway distance and you'd realize that you were still on earth."

The next time you drive to the corner store, think of Margie McCauley. Think of her, too, the next time you hunt for the closest parking space to the front door of the gym. Margie's feet did an amazing feat. She didn't just walk to the corner store or across a parking lot. She walked from Southern California to Chicago, Illinois. That's quite a trek for anyone, but Margie McCauley was in her 60s.

McCauley began her journey to follow Route 66 in 1995. She wasn't alone but her traveling companion couldn't offer a lot of conversation, unless Margie understood barking. McCauley's dog, Lollipop, or "Lolli" walked alongside as Margie pushed her three-wheeled cart. The first "leg" of the trip took the two of them and their combined six legs from California to Missouri. An accident with her cart badly damaged her leg and she went back to California to recuperate. The 67 year old McCauley, Lollipop, and the cart then picked up the trail in Missouri in '96 and they were on the road again, tracing the historic Route 66 and on their way to Chicago. I don't drive that far without a lot of planning and if you've driven America's open spaces you know there are times when you wish you could just bypass the miles and miles of endless horizon and get to your destination. Margie McCauley knew the feeling, but in at least one part of the country, it was just the opposite. I asked her if she got out in the middle of the Texas Panhandle and asked herself if she would ever get out of the area. "I enjoyed the Texas Panhandle...I want to tell ya' it was beautiful walking through there, much more beautiful than driving. I have driven through there and I'd always say, 'well, why can't I get out of this terrible place?' and walking through there, it was like being in space. You were the only person, you and your dog, alive, and you just look over and see the freeway distance and you'd realize that you were still on earth." She said "sensing so much more" is what keeps you going. "Being alive and also being a part of the earth."

That's not to say she didn't have moments when she was ready to give up. It hit her in nearly every state she was in, but, she remembered one time when she was in Oklahoma "and I was pushin' to get to a motel room that I thought that they had for me that night, and we had climbed hills all day." Ahead was "another great, terrible, terrible steep hill, and...I thought I could just sit here and cry and never move." Margie didn't want to lose the motel reservation and adds "the promise of that motel was stronger than my despair, so I said to Lolli, 'well, Lolli, sitting here crying is not going to get that hill climbed.'" So McCauley said, with her last shot of energy and a 70 pound cart, "we climbed a very short hill, but the steepest ever, and when we got there the motel room was already rented, but we lucked out. The motel owner had an old trailer he put us up in." It didn't have a shower, but she was able to wash up and sleep in a bed!

McCauley thought of Lolli as the star of the journey. When she got Lolli as a pup she had the idea of the trip but it wasn't until four years later they set out. Normally she kept pretty good control of the dog to keep her from going after a deer and over some steep embankment. One early morning Margie wasn't watching as closely and the dog quickly took off on her own after some jackrabbits, going over an embankment pulling their cart! Margie was yelling at the dog and had visions of losing her cart, stranding herself in the middle of nowhere. Lolli did finally stop, when she came up to a fence. The jackrabbits kept going. At first Margie was mad, then she laughed, figuring Lolli had to have her fun too.

Once in New Mexico a drunken man was trying to give a hug and Lolli bared her teeth and was ready to jump on him. That helped convince McCauley that with "God as our pilot" and Lolli's protection, the trip was meant to be.

When you drive a long distance you may pick the route based on stops every 200 miles but Margie gauged her trip on stops every ten or 15 miles. "Probably weather and traffic are my two worst enemies," she said. She couldn't always avoid the mountains either, and she agreed with me that even terrain that looks flat to a driver is not so flat to someone on foot, and a driver doesn't notice the subtle grade up and down. I suggested she had incredibly strong legs. "I just use 'em. I had never thought about how strong they were. They're not really muscular or anything. I just do it."

McCauley told me at the time Lollipop was doing very well but didn't really enjoy the walking. "I try to rest as often as I can and I try not to work her too hard." I thought maybe it was easier for the dog because Lollipop had four legs, but McCauley noted, "she has to take how many steps to my one?"

Margie's provisions on the cart included a stove, tent and sleeping bag as well as dried food, a form of an ice chest that might have had a Coke in it and perhaps some cheese and meat to give her and the dog some extra protein on the road. The cart also had a small flagpole including an American flag, a Christian flag and a flag from a Missouri football team, and of course a Route 66 flag made by a woman in Oklahoma.

It was easy to have McCauley talk to us at the radio station since our building was on the side of Route 66, about 60 miles southwest of her Chicago destination. She and Lolli pulled into our station parking lot and we did two interviews – one live, one taped for later. Coincidentally, the temperature at the time of her visit was an appropriate 66 degrees.

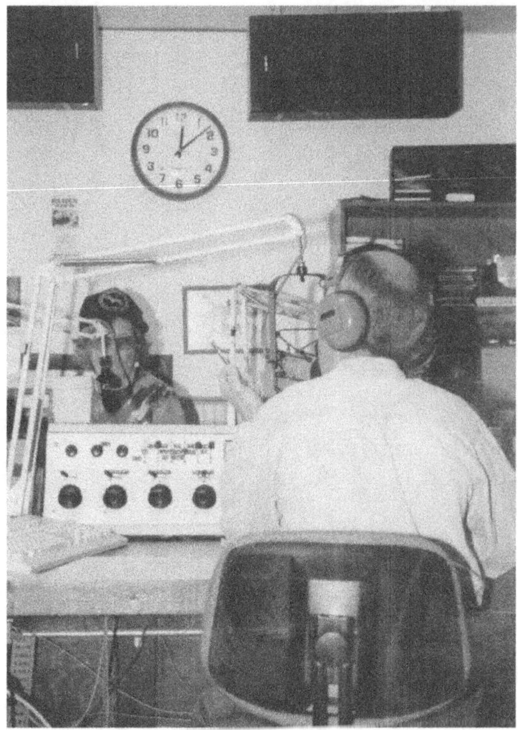

Her inspiration to go across country on foot came from a plan once to buy a RV and visit her sister in Connecticut. One day she told herself to take all that energy that she's given to everyone and her sense of adventure and take Lollipop on a walking/camping trip and "just whatever comes, you know and enjoy it." She was never a long distance walker but "walked a lot when I was a kid because we never had a car and my dad used to take me out for walks to the river on his day off. He was a postman," so she laughed when she said that may explain some of it.

She made it to Chicago and over a year later Margie wrote to us at the station to tell us how encouraging people in every state had been. She felt the best part of the trip had been from California to Missouri, because up until Illinois and points east she could toss her sleeping bag anywhere and "fend for myself." She was at her California home and telling us of the magnificent moon, bright stars and beautiful sky. Apparently her love of the open sky was as strong as her fascination with the open road. Margie McCauley has given new meaning to a "walk on the wild side."

WE WANT IT, YOU HAVE IT, WE DESERVE IT

AT SEVERAL RADIO stations, the job of Public Service Director fell to me and it can be frustrating. Many people and organizations want free airtime. I got requests for publicity at the last minute, requests for publicity that were hand scribbled, requests on posters and requests that came over the phone. Now, taking the information over the phone is risky. If they give the wrong time of the event, you have no proof who made the mistake. Or, what if it's a prank and you've just sent 200 people to a benefit or dance that doesn't exist? Get a hard copy for the file. The CYA theory -- Cover Your...uh...Alibi.

A lot of people have a cause and not all are from non-profit agencies because sometimes businesses doing something for the community want in on the free publicity. That's expected and it's sometimes a gray area whether the business is truly involved or truly greedy. Regardless, there is a right way and a wrong way to ask a person at the radio station to publicize your event. I've heard, "I need you to run our announcement, etc." "Need you to run," indeed! Even if it's not phrased that way, that's often the attitude. We at the station "owe" them. What they don't realize is that even the Federal Communications Commission stopped seeing it that way, removing any required amount of public service time for a radio station. Contrary to public perception, we were not a public utility.

Sometimes those wanting free airtime don't even bother to listen to the station or even give the appearance they listen. A caller will ask, "do you have a calendar of events? Would you publicize our...whatever?" They don't know what you have to offer but they want it for free. Radio stations are businesses and their commercial product is airtime. That's all they have to sell. So imagine it this way. What if I went to Walmart and said, "I don't know what you sell. Can I have a free lawn chair?"

Often a public service announcement or PSA, would come addressed innocuously, almost like "occupant." Make an effort to find out to whom you're writing. I say it again! Make an effort! One sports director I knew wouldn't even open an envelope that wasn't personally addressed to him. I didn't go that far, but I had been known to make a special effort to get a PSA on the air for someone because it was specifically addressed to me. I do get steamed about this, as you may have guessed by how fast I'm typing. Oh, yeah, you can't see that. Well, take my word for it. Thanks for letting me vent.

Obviously I enjoy interviews much more when it's a topic I enjoy and I've told you about my interest in collecting. I certainly enjoyed the topic as well as my talk with top autograph and manuscript expert Charles Hamilton. We spoke in November 1996, about a month before he died in what might have been his final radio interview. Autograph collecting is a tricky field with prices going up and down. It was Charles Hamilton's life work and believe it or not, autograph fakes and forgeries made the hobby and business more fun for him.

CHARLES HAMILTON

"I remember when Lincoln documents could be had for $15 or $20, but nobody was very much interested in Lincoln at that time. I used to sell baseballs signed by Babe Ruth for $15 and today they bring $5000."

What's in a name? Big business for some, big scams for others. That doodling you scribble on a pad as you talk on the phone isn't worth anything. If Picasso did the same thing, it would be framed and treasured. Recognizing bogus handwriting was the specialty of Charles Hamilton, regarded as one of the tops in his field of autographs and manuscripts. The author and handwriting expert died in December 1996. I talked with him in November of that year. Keep in mind the dollar figures have certainly changed since our interview many years ago. Hamilton told me autograph collecting had gone from something boys and girls did as a hobby to "an enormous business." He said, "the result is that the values of historic and literary and musical and scientific letters and documents have escalated to the point where collecting them is prohibitive to the average person." But he said, at the time, beginners were still able to have a lot of fun by writing to celebrities. However, he made it clear celebrities were mass-producing forgeries too. "Yes, indeed they are," he said in '96. "Especially celebrities like statesmen, astronauts, movie stars, baseball heroes. They all use a machine to sign their signatures now, or if they can't afford a machine they use a secretary."

Hamilton gained some of his fame by writing about President Kennedy and Kennedy's use of the Autopen to sign his name. The Autopen is a machine that can duplicate thousands of identical samples of the person's signature. It looks real until you find another exactly like it and realize, like a photostat, it's just a copy. But JFK didn't stop with that autograph duplicating machine. Besides a number of Autopen patterns, Hamilton said Kennedy had 18 secretaries who signed for him. You may think Hamilton would have been distraught over all of the forgeries, but he took pleasure in it and found it added to the interest and challenge. "If everything were genuine, where would be the fun in finding the real thing?" As Hamilton saw it, "it's the forgeries and the secretaries and the machines that make collecting so demanding, and I think so much more interesting."

Hamilton said a felt tip pen very effectively disguises a forgery. "It's so thick that all the fine lines and the fine movements and the fine touches of the actual handwriting are gone." He added, "the average ballpoint pen can do strange things too. It can skip at times or make a series of dots instead of a line, and these things all add to the general confusion of identifying authentic writings."

Hamilton never paid any attention to the history of the document, the so-called "provenance" that can accompany a piece, simply because he says it's easy to forge. For example, Hamilton said he noted rare Indian autographs such as those of Sitting Bull and Geronimo always came with a detailed provenance. He said the provenance would say how someone's grandfather was stationed at Fort Sill and he got the old Indian chief to sign his name. The latest owner will claim the signature was passed on to them with a statement, saying how the original collector was timid about approaching Sitting Bull, etc, etc. At the time of our interview Hamilton said, they all came with a statement like that, "forgetting that only 50 years ago, you could buy a Sitting Bull signature for a dollar and no sane person would ever accompany it with a certification of authenticity." Hamilton noted, "everybody says 'I got this signature of Babe Ruth in person when I was only ten years old,' and that's followed by a story of how Babe Ruth smiled and joked as he signed it and so on, and the ink is probably no older than two or three days and the forger has just finished it."

Hamilton felt as a collector, you have a right to believe what you're buying will increase in value, regardless of what you collect. His recommendation was to buy what you enjoy, and if you're a beginner, unless you're very wealthy, avoid specializing and collect everything that interests you. "It makes for a more exciting collection." You may not be able to afford an Abraham Lincoln signature, but he told me then that a signature of a member of Lincoln's cabinet could be bought quite cheaply.

Any investor knows the words "if only I'd bought then," and it applies to autograph collecting too. Hamilton said in our interview in 1996, "I remember when Lincoln documents could be had for $15 or $20, but nobody was very much interested in Lincoln at that time." As fashions change, so do values. As he said at the time, "25 years ago, nobody wanted baseball autographs and nobody wanted movie star autographs." Hamilton used to sell baseballs signed by Babe Ruth for $15 and when we talked in '96 he told me they brought $5000. Those numbers have probably changed, and not for the better for a tight budget.

Hamilton was amazed at that, but the change in fashion amazed him more. His advice to a young collector is "collect what nobody else wants." In our interview Hamilton said nobody seemed to be collecting signatures associated with the Arctic, "yet that's a coming part of world affairs." Another area at the time he found very interesting with increasing value was the field of African explorers. "Many other fields have hardly been touched at all. The trouble is that newcomers always want what is fashionable." He said when J.P. Morgan began collecting as a boy he picked the most fashionable of all autograph areas, Methodist Episcopal bishops, but "today (1996) you can't sell them at all." I laughed at that topic. It seemed rather obscure to me, but Hamilton pointed out that "at the time they were regarded as very great men." Good thing for J.P. Morgan his entire fortune wasn't tied up in that field.

He said most collectors of the 1850s and 1860s collected cabinet members because you could get a complete set and also members of the Continental Congress. But, at least in 1996, Hamilton said no one collected them. If you know the collecting hobby, you know the rarity and high price for the signature of Button Gwinnett, a signer of the Declaration of Independence. Years after our interview a signature could bring on average tens of thousands of dollars. You may be surprised to learn, as I was, that at one time, a member of the Continental Congress competed with Gwinnett's signature. But in 1996 Hamilton said that Continental Congress member's signature that once was as popular as Gwinnett's had dropped to a worth of only about $25. How's that for a fall from power, more than 200 years past his prime?

Hamilton said it was unfortunate the talk was all true about the incredible number of sports fakes. When we talked in 1996 he noted, "there are just tens of thousands of bogus sports autographs on the market, and the sellers of them are often heedless of whether or not they're genuine." He said some dealers didn't even want to handle them because they're so tough to authenticate. But crooks beware! Hamilton warned forgers there are ways to find whether the signatures are genuine. He told me he was working with the FBI and whenever they needed his help he gave it.

If some item came to him that he thought was faked by the person who brought it in, Hamilton would tell them, "I want to show you what a simple-minded half-wit can do when he tries to forge." He would say to the con artist, "can you imagine anyone with such pig knuckles for brains that he would endeavor to do this?" The crooks he's talked to didn't react well to that, "and I watch these forgers writhe."

Another approach he had was if someone brought in something Hamilton suspected had been stolen, he would tell the seller he had a potential buyer and to come back. Then Hamilton would call the police to be there to arrest the seller.

In our 1996 interview Hamilton told me the proliferation of forgeries, especially in the fields of movies and baseball was so extensive he doubted "whether even the most adroit and experienced experts of 25 or 50 years from now will be able to distinguish the genuine article from the fake." But Hamilton didn't have all bad news, believing there would be many fields of interest forgers would hesitate to attempt. "Today (in 1996) nobody tries to forge letters of Shelley and Keats, both of great value, but nobody tries it because it's so, so very easy to write the little signature of Lou Gehrig on a baseball and take it to a collector who is not knowledgeable, or a beginning dealer and say '...my father just died three weeks ago and I found this in one of his drawers and I can remember him telling me, vaguely I remember about how he met Lou Gehrig, but I never believed his story but I guess it must be true' and then on with the lies, lies, lies!"

Charles Hamilton died December 11, 1996, just over three weeks after our talk. I had joked with him that I had an original "Charles Hamilton" in my collection. That was from the time I wrote to him in the 1970s. He joked about being collected and didn't seem to take himself seriously when it came to the future value of his signature. When he died the next month, the autograph and collecting hobby and industry lost a great source of knowledge, integrity and humor.

In my long career in radio and communications I never got to interview Abe Lincoln. But I was close. I got to talk with David Herbert Donald, the Pulitzer Prize winning author of, believe it or not, "Lincoln." I was able to draw on Donald's extensive research into the makeup of our 16th president. If this were a tell-all bio of a modern president it might also explore the choice of TV makeup. But I digress again.

DAVID HERBERT DONALD

"He raced up and down the White House stairs, three stairs at a time...He enjoyed funny jokes with his secretaries. He liked his young wife who was ten years younger than he was and they had an active social life."

With this president it was the first time there had been little children in the White House and historian David Herbert Donald said, "they were rambunctious and a real trial, but he adored them." Donald said it was a different kind of White House with an active, vigorous, young president.

Donald said this president "raced up and down the White House stairs, three stairs at a time. He hallooed down the corridors. He enjoyed funny jokes with his secretaries. He liked his young wife who was ten years younger than he was and they had an active social life." You may think Donald was describing the John Kennedy or Teddy Roosevelt presidency, but maybe you're surprised to know he was talking about Abraham Lincoln. I tend to think of Lincoln as an older, almost grandfatherly president. But Donald pointed out Lincoln was only 51 when elected to the presidency and a man with "enormous physical vigor."

He said about Lincoln, "this is a guy who at the end of his life will go down to visit the troops near Fort Monroe, find some boys out there splitting logs with a heavy axe." Donald said Lincoln would tell the boys he used to do some of that and wanted to see if he still could. Lincoln borrows the axe and splits a couple of logs. "Then he takes the axe, again, maybe 12, 14 pounds, holds it out by the heft, the end of the handle, out straight, horizontal to the ground, and holds it there for ten seconds or so and lets it drop." As Lincoln leaves, Donald said the boys wonder whether they can repeat the feat. "These 16, 17, 18 year old boys pick up the axe and not a one of them can do it."

The author of "Lincoln" said when it came to Lincoln's fixed objectives there was no lack of clarity. "One was the Union had to be preserved at all costs. He never wavered for a moment on that. Second, once he got to the issue of emancipation he never again hesitated. Emancipation had to be the fixed terms of any peace arrangement." But Donald said Lincoln showed a great deal of flexibility in ways to reach these objectives. "Lincoln was a very adroit man. He realized that he did not have a majority of the country behind him. He was elected by a minority of the vote in 1860... He had no mandate, so he had to work cautiously and conservatively to build a consensus."

Donald added when Lincoln said he didn't have a policy what he meant was there wasn't a plan that went step A to step B. Lincoln's Republican Party was new to the national scene and Lincoln was not well acquainted in political circles. He didn't even know all of his cabinet members when they were appointed. Donald said Lincoln took things slowly to find his way.

The Great Emancipator was not an abolitionist. But Donald said you didn't have to be to oppose slavery. Donald noted, "one could say with the abolitionist, 'let's emancipate slaves right here and now, no compensation for the owners and get it over with.' Others could say, 'well, let's compensate the owners,' (and) others could say, 'let's do gradual emancipation.' Still others might say, 'well, let's try emancipation, providing that the slaves emancipated should be sent back to Africa or some other area.' These would be colonizationists. All of these are...varieties of anti-slavery people. The abolitionist was simply the most extreme, the most abstract of all of these groups. Lincoln was not an abolitionist. He was a cautious, anti slavery man who knew what could be done within the American Constitution."

Years ago the idea came up that Lincoln's Secretary of War, Edwin Stanton was behind the president's assassination, April 14, 1865. Donald said the idea has been challenged by historians and disproved, with one author pointing out there wasn't any reason for Stanton to be involved. Another misconception, according to Donald, is the belief that Lincoln had the genetic disorder called Marfan's syndrome. "It's characterized by extraordinarily long extremities, very long hands, very long feet and certainly Lincoln had very long hands and feet. I think he wore a size 14 shoe or something like that." As the problem progresses in midlife or beyond, symptoms include weakness and perhaps rupture of an aorta and then death. He says some looked at Lincoln's pictures and suspected the inherited ailment and then someone found some rather distant collateral relatives who did have Marfan's. "And so," Donald said, "putting things together they said, 'well, maybe Abraham Lincoln had Marfan's syndrome.'" He said, "we all got hot and bothered about this for a while. The National Museum of Medicine began an investigation. We do have enough blood stained pillows and scraps of Lincoln's hair that we could reconstitute his DNA and find out whether it showed the Marfan's syndrome gene." There was a conference and a push to pursue the matter. Then the idea began to cool. A Johns Hopkins University expert pointed out a DNA test for Marfan's was only about 50 percent accurate so whatever was found wouldn't mean much. Donald said the editor of the New England Journal of Medicine then asked a pertinent question. What good would it do to find the answer? Lincoln died from a bullet. That's when Donald said people began to realize it wasn't all that important. It was also about that time attention turned to the demise of Zachary Taylor and whether that president was poisoned.

As we talked in '96 Donald pointed out the question of Lincoln and Marfan's syndrome was no longer being asked. "We do not think now that Lincoln had Marfan's syndrome. There is no record of Marfan's syndrome among any of his lineal descendants, the last of whom...died fairly recently and we have no evidence that anybody inherited that gene from Abraham Lincoln."

Donald's favorite personal anecdote of Lincoln happened at the end of the Civil War. Generals Grant and Sherman met with the President near Fort Monroe and were discussing the nation's future and what to do with the captured Confederates. "Lincoln made it very clear he didn't want them to be captured but that for political reasons he couldn't say 'oh let 'em go, nothing to me. I want them out of the country.' Though he did say that he wouldn't care much if they escaped." Lincoln told a joke and Donald said, "in those days everybody told ethnic jokes. They usually were Irish jokes." Donald quoted Lincoln as saying he was like the Irishman who had a drinking problem. His neighbors had told the man he must not drink anymore. "And so the Fourth of July parade was coming on and the Irishman was standing in the bar and he told the bartender, 'give me a lemonade,' he said. The bartender, looking surprised, said, 'you sure you don't want a dram of the spirits in it?' And the Irishman said to him, 'well,' he said, 'you know, if you could put a little whiskey in there, unbeknownst to me, I wouldn't mind.' Well, Lincoln liked to have things done unbeknownst to him and he made it clear repeatedly that he didn't himself want to be involved in the dirty nitty gritty of politics or even of decisions about the Confederates." But Donald said, if it were "unbeknownst to him he wouldn't mind and he would not have minded had all the Confederates fled the country to Europe and never been heard of again."

PRESIDENTS ARE LIKE BUSES. WAIT LONG ENOUGH AND ANOTHER WILL BE ALONG

IT HAD BEEN years since I had covered President Ronald Reagan at that 1984 reelection rally in Sacramento in front of the California Capitol. Now, his successor was campaigning for reelection in 1992 by coming to the military base side of O'Hare Airport in Chicago to attend a Polish festival. I was at the arrival spot on the tarmac as the relatively new and impressive blue and white Air Force One 747, serial number 28000, pulled up and both George H.W. and Barbara Bush came down the steps.

It's the same plane his son George W. would fly around the country during the unsettled hours of September 11, 2001. Officially this was a closed arrival with no public rally. But there were some people, military types and I suppose their families. This was a campaign trip in September of 1992 so you'd think George would make every effort to greet those who had come to see him. Nope, not even a wave hello. Just get in the limo and leave. You probably remember he lost that election to Bill Clinton.

Print reporters can get pictures. TV can roll video. With radio I'm limited to the roar of the jet and then have to do a story by interviewing some of the crowd who get to see a president, some for the first time. It's a technique that worked well for me and about my only option when I attended presidential photo opportunities such as arrivals and departures.

At that same spot on the airport tarmac two years later Bill Clinton flew in aboard one of those beautiful blue and white 747s that are the cream of the presidential fleet. But he came over to greet the crowd.

While Clinton was friendlier he seemed to bring the confusion that was often tied to his whole administration in the early days. I had arranged to pick up my press credentials for the visit when I arrived at O'Hare, rather than travel all the way into a Chicago press office from the outer suburbs to get them. When I got to the airport, the Secret Service guy said they didn't even have a press office in Chicago. I admit I didn't remember the name of the press person I had spoken to, and that was my mistake and maybe I confused the issue. Regardless I waited and waited and finally the Secret Service came over and said I was cleared to go in to the area. That didn't mean an automatic place on the press flatbed trailer but I had no trouble climbing up on that. As it turned out, though, the best "seats" so to speak, would have been in the crowd as Clinton moved along the line shaking hands.

Helicopter "Marine One" waits next to "Air Force One" at Chicago O'Hare Airport military section to fly Bill Clinton

Again, in what had become my "get a presidential story when I don't have anything to talk about mode," I interviewed crowd members after Clinton left.

I wrote a letter complaining about the mess up over the credentials and to her credit, even as she was preparing to leave her job, Clinton Press Secretary Dee Dee Meyers (or maybe a staffer who wrote her signature) took the time to write to me and apologize.

If you've been to a presidential visit that's designed for public consumption, you know how impressive the "show" can be. Far different from a mere candidate's arrival.

During Clinton's 1996 reelection campaign, he came to a suburban Chicago high school. Picture this scene. Next to the school is a small lake with a park-like setting. Clinton's helicopter, along with two other helicopters swoop in. (Can a helicopter swoop? Maybe not, but it is a colorful description.)

Bill Clinton and his entourage landing at Homewood-Flossmoor High School in Flossmoor, Illinois

The helicopters land just out of sight. Then a motorcade appears with two Cadillac limousines and flags on the fenders as the President is driven the short distance around the lake and over to the entrance to the speaker's area. Now that's pomp and ceremony. Compare that to a simple candidate who has to charter a plane and rent a limo.

Before Clinton arrived on the speaker's stand an aide placed the round presidential seal on the front of the lectern. How often do you see that in the official or network coverage?

Clinton did seem to like to work a crowd. After his speech, he left the platform, went back up on it to cross to the band members and continued campaigning. I seem to remember noticing the glint of Clinton's wedding ring. I paid attention to it. In 1996 I'm not sure he did.

Clinton would say his problems were personal, not public. That's a matter of debate.. One fictional TV family that would have had a tough time under the spotlight of the media would be the family headed by Gomez and Morticia Addams. But then, come to think of it, they were in the spotlight every week and now all the time in reruns and remakes. Radio had once again given me the chance to talk with a cultural household name, the original Gomez Addams, known in the real world as talented actor John Astin.

JOHN ASTIN

"Gomez really, in a lot of ways, is just an extension of my own personality."

No matter what actor John Astin accomplished, he will probably always be mainly known as the head of a creepy and kooky, mysterious and spooky, altogether ooky collection of television oddballs called the Addams Family. Astin was the patriarch, Gomez Addams, and you may remember Carolyn Jones as Morticia, Jackie Coogan as Uncle Fester, Ted Cassidy as Lurch and family members Grandmama, Wednesday, Pugsley and of course Thing – as himself. Astin became a veteran character actor who began his show biz career in the 1950s and went on to perform in TV, plays and movies, running the gamut from the movie, "West Side Story" to the Riddler in the TV show "Batman." He was Buddy, Harry Anderson's wacky father in the TV hit, "Night Court." Remember his catchphrase in that show? "I'm feeling much better now." If you have a real grasp of trivia, you may be aware of his character Harry Dickens in the 1962 TV series "I'm Dickens, He's Fenster." Despite his decades in the business when we talked in 1997 it didn't bother Astin that he was best known for the role of Gomez Addams. He said then, "even though it was done a long time ago and it only occupied a limited chunk of my career, the show has never really been off the air in all that time and so in a strange way it's almost a current show." He laughed when he admitted he liked watching it. "I haven't seen it for quite a while," he told me, "but when I do see it, I must confess I enjoy it." He said the Addams had a pretty good home life, adding "Gomez really, in a lot of ways, is just an extension of my own personality, so it was pretty easy to do, in that sense, once the character was developed and conceived and thought about enough." Astin readily agreed Gomez Addams certainly had a 'joie de vie' – a joy of life -- that was "probably the core of the character, " and Astin considered it very much a part of the show. When we talked, he was doing a stage show playing poet Edgar Allan Poe, a man who had similarities to Gomez Addams. "Poe's approach to life was one of enormous appreciation for the wonder and the depth of life." That was in spite of the tragedy and difficulties in Poe's life. You may be surprised, but Astin says Poe had a wonderful sense of humor. He saw Poe as "one of the most exciting minds and personalities we've ever had." Gomez Addams also appreciated Poe and quoted from him occasionally.

According to Astin, the "Addams Family" actors' ensemble worked well together. "We were just a very compatible cast." He adds, "we had a lot of professional respect for one another, plus personal liking and it extended throughout the cast." They also all loved the show. "None of us felt the show was something we wouldn't want to be doing. All of our hearts were in it and we had a good time."

Most of the principals in the show were veteran actors by the time they moved into the creepy old Addams mansion. Astin said, "Carolyn Jones was already well-established and Jackie Coogan obviously had been, at one time, the most popular star in Hollywood. But, of course, times change." Astin told me there were times he had to explain to people who Jackie Coogan was, "and why I say he was so popular." Coogan was born in 1914 and died in 1984. He was acting as early as 1919 and his roles included everything from the title role in "The Kid" in 1921 to a performance in 1992, eight years **after** he died. That appearance and addition to his long resume was because film footage of Coogan was used in the 1992 movie, "Chaplin." You've seen Coogan on shows ranging from the "Brady Bunch" and "The Partridge Family" to "Gunsmoke" to "The Andy Griffith Show," to "Wild, Wild West" and "Police Story." Coogan's credits go on for pages, covering nine decades, but along the way, of course, Coogan was Uncle Fester in the "Addams Family" from 1964 to 1966.

Astin was on the stage in his early career but he said he didn't necessarily prefer stage work. He said at the time, "I love it all. I just go where the material is, really." When "Batman" was a TV show, Astin played "The Riddler." He said it was a cool thing to be in "Batman," which he adds, "was always a hot show." He remembered, "when they called me up, you know, I said, 'Frank Gorshin is doing "The Riddler," isn't he?'" They told Astin not now he wasn't. "I never knew why and I said 'well, okay.'" You know I had always wanted to run around in my underwear," so he did the show. "Had a ball." That's despite the fact that "occasionally that outfit did itch a bit, but it was fun. I got a kick out of it." A perhaps little known bit of trivia – one of his Riddler henchman in the episodes he did was Lefebvre, former Chicago Cubs manager, who was then a second baseman for the Los Angeles Dodgers.

A lot of situation comedies drew their stars from standup comedy, but that wasn't Astin's background. He said "getting classical training (as an actor) to begin with, was, I think, very important for me. I think it helped me in almost everything I did. Gomez, I think, was helped by my classical training and all the, you know, the Shakespeare and Moliere and Greek plays that I did. I think that kind of training is very, very good for actors."

Actors and celebrities will probably always have to deal with the tabloids, but years ago Astin came up with a way to stay out of them. If they wrote something untrue about him, his plan was to have a lawyer write a letter to them that says, "you're writing a story that says XYZ. It's not true and it's damaging to me. So if you reprint that story or this letter we will assume you've done it with malicious intent, because we're telling you it's gonna' hurt us and so we will proceed accordingly." And they respond to that? "Oh sure," says Astin, "because you're nailing the thing right down. You're saying 'this is a lie. You're damaging me by printing a lie, therefore we will consider that you're proceeding with malicious intent.' It's establishing malicious intent." Astin added, "that's the hard thing for any damages. You can win a case or get a retraction or something, but ultimately that doesn't do you any good and doesn't teach them a lesson or stop them, really, because it doesn't cost them anything. You have to hit them in the pocket." Said Astin, "we were out of the tabloids in a flash."

Astin loved his character of Harry Anderson's father, Buddy Ryan, in the TV show "Night Court." "I'd love to do a series with that character," he told me in our 1997 interview. When I told him I had just seen him on an episode of "Love Boat" it prompted him to talk about the extra special treatment actors got from producer Aaron Spelling. The episode I saw was filmed in Egypt. Astin loved the experience. "Boy, that was wonderful to do. I mean we were there a month. It was like a month's vacation almost...What an incredible trip that was! Very exciting." He said when we talked, "it's always wonderful to work for Aaron Spelling. He pays you well. He goes first class and then, by George, you've gotten a paid vacation from Aaron, and then he sends you a gift afterwards. I mean, what more could you ask for?" Astin described Spelling as "a first class fellow." Spelling died in 2006.

As a radio person, as I've mentioned, I ask notable people to do a promotion for me, those so-called "liners." Astin graciously agreed, but my request posed that problem I told you about. I had hoped he would tie the liner into his Gomez Addams catchphrase. When Morticia said something in French, Gomez responded by saying "Tish, when you speak French, you drive me wild!" But similar to what Tom Bodett told me about his catchphrase, Astin didn't own the "Addams Family" show and was concerned about stepping across legal lines by saying the phrase for me. He hit on a compromise after he learned my last name is an Italian name. We were discussing how to pronounce Jannuzzi and he spoke Italian. I was impressed that he knew there was no J in the Italian alphabet. Originally my name began with an "I." So one of his liners to me was "I'm John Astin...and when I hear that name Jannuzzi, it drives me wild. Ah, but you have to say it Iannuzzi (EE ann ootz ee). That's the correct way."

After the interview we got into a discussion about my Italian family roots and he seemed genuinely intrigued. I've felt affection for Gomez Addams for years. I was glad to connect for a few minutes with the man behind that lovable character, John Astin, who I found to be a really classy guy himself.

IS THERE A SCHOOL FOR PUBLIC FIGURING?

MOST OF THE public figures I've talked to are nice, even if being nasty makes a better story, but, of course, nice and/or personable is part of what gets them some success. (So what's my excuse?)

You try to get a glimpse of a celebrity or notable person as they might be in their living room, except without the socks on the floor. But, of course, sticking a microphone in someone's face is not always a natural experience, for them at least. It can be intimidating, though probably not usually for a celebrity, for whom in most cases I would think a mic would be a chance for a "performance." As I mentioned in the introduction, in one sense everyone is performing or selling himself or herself when you interview them. Some are just better at it.

One of the highest compliments I could get from an interviewee was to be told, "I've never been asked that question." I'm proud to have broken new ground, sailed uncharted water, blazed new...well, you get the idea.

Politicians, on the other hand, have their own facade and probably should have their own chapter. They can be a tough shell to crack. I knew a now former congressman who was so good at wearing his political face, he was probably destined for prominence. Ask him his opinion and he'd word it to tell you what he wants you to know, even if it's not necessarily the question you asked. This is not a new technique for politicians but it is effective in protecting political talking points. It can be very frustrating. He'd spout the party line and work it into the next answer too. Unfortunately that's a successful method in today's political world, for these "faux plain speakers," to get a message across.

One actual and real plain speaker, a man who told you pretty directly what he meant, was actor James Gregory. Both politicians and actors have a public face. As a character actor Jim Gregory had many faces but I could never call him two faced. He seemed to be the genuine article.

JAMES GREGORY

"I also, but keep this quiet, Biff -- I slept in Marilyn Monroe's bed."

If you watched television in the 1960s or 1970s you saw James Gregory. He was in more than 200 television shows and over 30 movies. The career of this New York-born actor spanned five decades.

This man was everywhere, from "Twilight Zone" to "Bonanza," from "Star Trek" to "That Girl" to "Columbo" to "Quincy" and from "Mission Impossible" to "M*A*S*H*" Perhaps his best known television role was the rough edged, but lovable, Inspector Frank Luger in "Barney Miller." His movie credits include the role of General Ursus in "Beneath the Planet of the Apes" and Senator Iselin in "The Manchurian Candidate." James Gregory was Elvis' father in the 1967 movie, "Clambake" and played Morgan Hastings in "The Sons of Katie Elder" with John Wayne. Gregory appeared in several "Matt Helm" movies with Dean Martin and his resume goes on for pages. Gregory didn't have a favorite part he had played. He told me, "no, that's like saying 'who's your favorite actor' and you're going to offend somebody." He said actors have answered that question by saying, "the next one." I laughed and started another question. Didn't get far when he stopped me. "That's a joke. Wait for the laugh." At the time of our phone interview in 1996, Gregory, at age 84, was living in the beautiful Red Rock country of Sedona, Arizona. I asked if there were another part to play in his future. "I don't think so, Biff…I don't feel I could give 100 percent. However, I have left a couple of hooks with bait on them dangling and saying if you want an elderly gentlemen who walks with a cane and speaks a little differently, let me know, we'll make a deal."

Gregory was still getting letters with photos from his appearance in "Star Trek" asking him to autograph the pictures. He was surprised at the "tremendous interest in the sci-fi things." Along with that, he said, goes the sci-fi movie, "Beneath the Planet of the Apes" and the requests for pictures of him in his role as General Ursus, "in the ape outfit." Because the makeup was so extensive for that role, Gregory was required to be in the makeup chair about 4:30 in the morning to be ready for an 8:30 shoot. Gregory says some people think the role of General Ursus was his greatest performance, but that's not how he sees it. For him it was just another job.

Gregory credited the success of "Barney Miller" not only to the TV show's regulars, but the wonderful actors who came in as featured characters week after week. He didn't think of the show as a "sitcom" but preferred to describe it as a "char-com" focusing on the characters.

It was a fun cast but he said "not hilarious, like some of these people nowadays that talk about 'oh we had such fun. He was so marvelous.' Nothing like that. We had our sly, dry humor and as the show progressed…the writers would write more or less for you as you had established (the character)."

When we talked in the 1990s, situation comedies annoyed Gregory because of the use of canned laughter. Maybe it bothers you too. Gregory added, "you're to laugh at every line and they have the sound machine there laughing hilariously. If somebody says 'I think I'll go home for dinner,' (imitating the canned laugh) Ahhohohohohohoho! And that revolts me. It insults my intelligence."

You've seen the technique where a show's credits are pushed to one side of the TV screen while a commercial airs on the other half. Gregory thought that was a cheap practice. "We fought too long for certain rights, the Screen Actors Guild and AFTRA, to put up with that kind of nonsense."

While on the set of the movie "Clambake," Elvis Presley commented he was quite impressed with Gregory's performance in the 1959 movie "Al Capone" with Rod Steiger. Gregory thought it was one of the best Capone films made. Elvis watched it when he was in the Army in Germany. When Presley and Gregory were on the set of "Clambake," Gregory says, "(Elvis) used to greet me every morning, 'good morning Mr. Gregory, sir.' After about three mornings I said to him, 'Elvis,' I said, 'we're gonna' be together a few weeks on the picture now, so it's not necessary for you to say good morning, Mr. Gregory, sir. Just say 'Jim.' That's fine, that's good enough,' I said." Gregory laughed as he recalled coming in the next morning and Elvis said, "good morning Mr. Jim, sir." That was a sign of Elvis's upbringing. "It amused me." Gregory remembered Elvis as "a real down to earth young fellow. Too bad he got fouled up the way he did." Gregory recalled Elvis "had quite an entourage always around the show, you know, while we were making the picture and then we had a tremendous wrap party." He added, "for a movie named "Clambake" they had "all the finest fixin's of seafood and other delicacies. It was a pleasant experience."

When Gregory worked on the "Matt Helm" films he found Dean Martin "very easy to get along with." Martin "took everything in his stride. He didn't get intense." and Gregory remembers 'Dino' as a good actor and a nice man.

Gregory got involved in barbershop quartet singing and into his 80s still considered himself a good singer. He was a booster of the international group called the Society for the Preservation and Encouragement of Barbershop Quartet Singing in America or SPEBSQSA, and had been a member for 25 years. I asked him to sing and he obliged. When he finished Gregory jokingly pushed for a bigger reaction from me. "Knock, knock, ya' still there?" he asked, adding. "I did that off the top of my head because I love ya' and then you give me no reaction." He sang the last line again. This time I applauded and said I knew our audience was applauding too. "You can dub in something," he joked.

The character of General Iron Guts Kelly on the television show "M*A*S*H*" died in what Gregory described as "a questionable association" with Loretta Swit's character "Hotlips." When the director came in for the closer shot, Gregory suggested "I could just put a little satisfied, subtle smile on my face. I thought it would be a nice end to the scene." But the director from England couldn't quite accept what Gregory was getting at, "but of course the general expired after a capitulation." He told me this during our radio interview and maybe had some concern. "Are you allowed to say that on the air?" I told him I thought we were okay with that.

James Gregory said he didn't watch himself on TV much. He'd watch occasionally if a fan sent something from the far distant past. One fan sent a "Rawhide" episode Gregory did with Clint Eastwood years ago but "I don't make a point if I have seen it. I have videos of a couple of movies that I've done, but they are more or less for posterity." He joked, "posterity. Do you know her?" Suddenly we were doing a routine. "There was an intermarriage there, cousins..." adding, "those are the jokes."

He was sent a copy of "The Manchurian Candidate," when the film was re-released. It's about political assassination. "You know, it was released once and then (President) Kennedy was assassinated and so they pulled it. They thought it bad taste."

Sometimes actors get together by chance. Gregory boasted he acted in a movie with Greta Garbo -- sort of. After World War Two he was making a film on New York's Madison Avenue about security in the Army, and when they viewed the film, there was Greta Garbo in the background with her dark glasses looking in a store window. "So I can always say I was in a film with Greta Garbo." In a half whisper, Gregory also told me he once slept in Marilyn Monroe's bed. How did that happen? "I was hoping you'd ask," he said. Gregory explained that one time he was in Hollywood about to register at the Chateau Marmont, a popular place for actors to stay. "Arthur Miller and Marilyn had just checked out and we had checked into the same apartment in the Chateau Marmont so I can always say I slept in Marilyn Monroe's bed."

I'll let James Gregory end the interview with the words of his "Barney Miller" character, Inspector Luger. "See ya' later, Barney. Toot Toot."

Milton Berle has the title of Mr. Television, but James Gregory has the resume.

I think Steve Allen used to say, "all seriousness aside," and one guy who understood the glamour and the pressure of show biz was musician, saxophonist David Sanborn. It can't be easy in any field to reach the level of recognition he's gained and harder still, to maintain it. Talking to him was a treat, and I don't even play a musical instrument, but I do love jazz.

DAVID SANBORN

"There are people who get a little peevish when you cast the net wide...Everybody has their own definition of what jazz really is. I think people just need to lighten up."

Saxophonist David Sanborn said in our 1997 interview if you were an up and coming musician there weren't the opportunities you would have had perhaps 20, 30 years before to start in the small clubs and work your way up. But Sanborn, who began his career in St. Louis clubs, told me "the landscape is always changing and I think if you're really serious about wanting to be a musician, nothing's gonna' stop you. You're gonna' play because you have to play."

As I've mentioned, as an interviewer/talk show host I took my interviews where I got them. David Sanborn was available to me in 1997 because he was pitching a product he felt would be useful for wind instrument players suffering from cold sores on the lips. I was happy to get that plug in for him, but also pleased he would talk about his career. I'm sure he knew the carrot to get radio interviewers to talk about the product was his celebrity and the chance to talk with him. I took advantage of it and among other questions asked him about the complaint that jazz was given too wide a definition. Sanborn's attitude was more relaxed about it. "There are people who get a little bit peevish when you cast the net wide...It's a very hard kind of music to describe. Everybody has their own definition of what jazz really is. I mean, I think people just need to lighten up," as he laughed. "I mean, there's room for everybody out there."

Sanborn's resume includes a number of Grammy awards and had been a solo artist since 1975. At one time he played regularly with Paul Shaffer, bandleader for "Late Night With David Letterman" on the show. I asked Sanborn if Shaffer pretty much had control, or if all of the musicians could contribute. He told me the "Late Night" show had a dynamic of its own, so in a sense you kind of had to follow the program." Sanborn said the way it worked was that Shaffer called the tunes and it was "actually kind of like a "Name That Tune" situation a lot." He said everyone might know the tune but nobody had rehearsed it so it was a "kind of a fly by the seat of your pants situation."

Had Sanborn reached a level where he could pretty much pick and choose the people he worked with? He wondered if anybody had that total freedom, but in our '97 interview he told me he felt very comfortable with the options he had in his professional life. "Being a leader of my own group I can pretty much choose the kinds of venues that I play and I have a lot of options open to me where I'll play some concerts with symphony orchestras, and I'll play a certain kind of music with that, in that context, and then I'll play electric music and then I'll play a more acoustic music for other situations. So there's a lot of flexibility there."

One of his trademarks was playing different styles. But he said in our 1997 talk it didn't require different muscles or windpower. "I think it's just a mental process. There are probably certain adjustments that you make, but I think at this point it's very unconscious for me and if I do make them I'm not aware of them, if I'm playing jazz. I mean, generally when you're playing acoustic music the dynamic range is much wider, and you can play in the softer volumes and the lower level so you can exploit a different character of the saxophone than when you're playing more kind of high energy, hard edge electric music.

There was a downside to the level of success he reached. "I guess it's just the kind of personal pressure that you put on yourself. I think you're more or less competing with yourself. You want to do better than you did last time if you're looking at the next record and I think it's all self imposed."

I asked in '97 if music were still as much fun for him? "Absolutely. I have no choice about doing anything else right now. I don't think I ever did. I think maybe at one point it was either this or steal cars."

When we talked, he said composing was still a major part of his work and he admitted it's a more solitary action. "Yeah it is, so I kind of run the gamut of the kind of context I work in, the more solitary and also the more public."

I also asked him if there were anyone he hadn't played with whom he wanted to work with. "You know that's a good question and I'm often asked that and I can never think of anybody. I always think of somebody like about a half an hour later." I suggested he call back in a half an hour. He laughed and said he'd do that. I'm still waiting, David. Of course I've changed my number many times since that conversation. Maybe that's the delay.

VE HALF VAYS TO MAKE YOU TALK

IT ALWAYS SURPRISED me that people were so willing to give interviews. I don't know if it's an ego trip for them, but when I ask if they'd mind talking into a recorder, they usually agree. Isn't that amazing? It can be very frustrating, though, when you finish an interview that has been a bit like pulling teeth and then once the mic is off, the words flow and the interviewee is saying what you'd been trying to get out of them for ten minutes. Or someone is nervous at the start of a long interview show, giving short answers. Then once you get near the end you have to start watching your time carefully because by now they're warmed up and the spigot is running on and the clock is running out and there's a collision a'comin' and you'd better jump aside! Actually if you're the conductor you just take a firm hand and stop that interview before someone is a'killed!

It's odd, but body language can help too. If I poise a finger on the electronic controls or shift my position, it seems to jar loose some awareness from the interviewee that it's time to move on.

Speaking of unspoken code, of which I speak, sometimes not speaking can trigger a longer and better answer. What do I mean by this? Let me ask the questions, please! When asking an interview question, and you want someone to elaborate, let them give their answer and then just say nothing to them. People find the silence awkward and sometimes will fill the gap and you'll get more for your interview dollar.

I'm sure you have your own pet peeves in your work. For me a big one was like fingernails on a chalkboard when I heard broadcasters, "broadcasting," using phrases like, "good afternoon, everyone" and "how is everyone doing?" My point is how often have you listened to radio in a group? Radio is usually **one on one**. When a broadcaster uses general terms like that it sets up a psychological wall between the listener and the radio. It diffuses what should be a very personal connection between the broadcaster and you. To show what I mean, imagine sitting in a living room with one friend and every time you say something to the person across the couch you speak as if there were hundreds of people in the room. "Have any of you read any good books lately? Did all of you like that new movie?" Your friend would give you a strange look and it would hardly sound like a personal conversation with just one person.

I also get very upset at the word "very" because it's very often redundant. "Now here's our reporter with the "very" latest." Aargh! Either it's the latest or it's not. I wish that phrase was "very" dead. That's not my "very" only gripe. As long as I'm ranting and raving, how about the use of "later today" or "earlier yesterday." Sometimes you have to qualify the time to make sure the listener or reader understands the timeline of events. But mostly using those phrases is just lazy. Obviously the announcement will come later today so just say "will come today." Why "earlier" yesterday? If it's yesterday it had to be earlier. And what's up with "traveling northbound" or "traveling southbound?" He was traveling either north or south! But perhaps I'm getting carried away, or traveling off the deep end...northbound.

IT'S PR, NOT NEWS AND DON"T CONFUSE THE TWO

AT ONE POINT in my career, between radio station jobs, I helped form a community promotional newspaper to pitch businesses and promote some good things happening in the area. I'll tell you, though, after working hard news and even feature news for years, to shift to all public relations writing is an odd mental switch. There's a place for that type of writing, but I quickly realized it isn't as intellectually honest. When I write, for example, about a business, I may want to ask about the negative side of a story, but with a promotional piece that won't fly. Once a couple got a slot on my show for 30 minutes to talk about one of those diet supplements. I explained it would not be an infomercial, but apparently they were upset when the questioning was not as "softball" as they had hoped. At one point I questioned the importance of their claim the product was natural by pointing out marijuana is natural too, but that doesn't mean it's good for you. Once James Randi made a similar point speaking about the definition of natural and he noted bird droppings are natural but he wouldn't want to eat them.

Moving to promotional print copy I also had to get used to the length of stories. In a radio story I could often remember most of what I need for the story. Print stories are paragraphs and paragraphs, as you can see. The worst part is I had to ask someone how to spell their name! When I was writing radio copy for myself, I never worried about that. In my radio copy, as long as it sounded right, it could stay in, unless of course I wrote for another anchor.

You may think I would only choose to work at a radio station where I liked the music. I didn't have that luxury and liking a format had little to do with whether I would do news for a station. But it does make it easier to keep the car radio turned on if the format doesn't make me gag. Even if it were an "All Country Polka, All the Time" format that would be okay if we had the audience.

SURE IT'S THE BOTTOM OF THE FOOD CHAIN. BUT IT'S SHOW BIZ

RADIO IS SHOW biz, or at least I've always thought of it that way, but doing TV and movie work as an extra? Now this was something new. You've heard the joke about the guy who gets the "glamorous" job of following the elephant in the circus parade with a shovel. He's asked why he doesn't quit and he answers, "what, and give up show business?" Well, being an extra on a TV show or movie has some of the same features. But it can be wonderful too. An extra is the bottom of the food chain. You can spend hours waiting, just to be on the set for ten minutes. Then you still may not get camera "face time," as I liked to call it.

But I wanted to try it out so through my friend Bob Erck (now maybe he'll buy a book since his name is here) I learned how to register with a casting agency for the Chicago area for the TV show "Early Edition." It's on DVD now and is about a guy who gets the "Chicago Sun-Times" delivered by a mysterious cat a day early so he always knows and tries to prevent the "disaster du jour" and a couple more too.

The first time I worked on the show it was as a cook at McGinty's, the fictional restaurant/bar owned by the series lead played by Kyle Chander.

That 12 hours at the set of "Early Edition" resulted in about three seconds of me from the elbow down. Guess you could call that "elbow time." I was upstaged by a cat, the cat, the one who gets a lot of "face time." He wasn't even in this scene but supposedly the show's lead character was looking for him and so the camera was looking toward the floor, cutting my upper body out of the shot, the feline ham. My friend Bob and I did get to visit briefly with Tim Kazurinsky of "Saturday Night Live," and "Police Academy" movie fame and if you're a real trivia buff, he was the photographer in the love story "Somewhere In Time." Normally you're not supposed to talk with the stars. I suppose it distracts them from being "in character," but this was next to the food table and I suppose was down time for him. I playing a cook and was wearing the double-breasted cook or chef's jacket. Wonder if he thought I worked for the caterers?

The second "extra" stint for "Early Edition was also 12 hours of work, this time at the Chicago Field Museum. The plot centered on an Egyptian exhibit and a statue of a cat (is there a theme here?) with the ability to put a curse on the person who takes the gems that are its eyes.

I was supposedly a partygoer at the museum's fundraiser. This time I spent more time standing around on the set so I got to see a lot more, but still only got about three seconds "face time" when the show aired. To tell you the truth, if it had been a bank surveillance camera on a robbery, they would not have been able to pin anything on me! You had to know where to look, but I did spot me in the overhead shot of the fundraising event. After the casting agency's fee and taxes I took home about $50. That's about $15 per second on air. Plus a couple of free meals.

My second TV show and third stint as an extra came on the show about a family of Chicago police officers headed by the patriarch, actor William Devane. His credits include "Knots Landing," "The Missiles of October," where he played JFK, the movie "Hollow Man" and even a recurring role as the father of Kyle Chandler on TV's "Early Edition." He seemed a rather colorful guy, joking on the set, yet not really outgoing behind the scenes. Maybe he was concentrating in the very little time I spent around him. There is big money involved in making a TV show and too much diversion can cost time and money.

It was exciting to be up close and personal with national television production work. "Turks" was often set in a Chicago bar called Emmit's. Now that I've been on the set and in the real bar it was patterned after, it amazed me how close the two were in appearance.

One of the bartenders at the real Emmit's was also a waitress in the TV show. In the real Emmit's you could go through one door and be in the kitchen. In the fake Emmit's going through that same door would put you in a woodshop area. Go through a side door in the real bar and you'd have been on the sidewalk. The same door on the set would get you...well, just behind the set.

There was a row of windows above the booths in the fake bar just as there was in the real setting but the window view out the fake bar was more attractive. Maybe that's because the show's crew could pick the scene for the backdrop. The folks at the real Emmit's were pretty much stuck with the background Chicago gave them. In the fake Emmit's the view was a huge color picture of a street scene with excellent perspective, at least until some people were standing between the set and the backdrop photo. Then it threw the perspective out of whack and the people looked like giants.

If you weren't in a scene you might be doing crossovers past the camera. You would wait for a production person to signal you and you'd cross perpendicular to the camera. You weren't recognizable because you were just a blur giving a sense of motion to the room scene. It looks pretty real on camera too.

The crew isn't too particular though about every placement of an extra. I guess there isn't time to have someone new in each scene. In one scene I was filmed in three spots and two showed up on camera, for the same scene. First I was seated at a bar table, then I was standing near the bar, then I was back at the table. The third angle and the one they didn't use was me walking past the guest star. In that same episode, my friend Bob was behind the lead actress and when they cut to William Devane for his reaction to her, Bob was in the background of that shot too.

My third TV show I worked was "Cupid," a well acted, cleverly written show about a man played by Jeremy Piven, who thinks he's Cupid and feels it's his duty to match lovers. The character of his psychiatrist friend didn't quite see it that way. In the episode I was on, it was a reworking of the plot of "Man of LaMancha" the show titled "Grand Delusions." A disturbed man thought he was Don Quixote and had fallen in love with a bar stripper, his "Dulcinea." Piven, as "Trevor Hale" AKA "Cupid," tried to fix him up.

As extras on this episode we were told to dress sleazy. You're usually told to bring a change or two of clothes and the style to wear. On "Turks" I was a cop in a bar so a pullover sweatshirt worked just fine. On "Cupid" this day I wore some worn pants and a denim jacket with a white fleece collar. Somehow I was picked to do a scene at the strippers' runway in the bar with Piven and actress Daphne Ashbrook, who played the stripper. I guess I had the right amount of sleaze. This was the late '90s and I knew who Piven was from the "Ellen" show and looked forward to seeing him. I had not seen a script, but extras, as you know now, are not important. At one point Piven started tossing lines at me to the effect that was I still on the vice squad and he knew my wife. The idea was that his character was trying to embarrass me to get me to leave the bar so he could talk to the stripper. As he delivered the lines I smiled and nodded, not understanding the context, but he came up later and explained that wouldn't be the right reaction. So finally I got it right and reacted with embarrassment that I was in the bar and bolted from the chair. We did the scene a number of times from several angles. It was fun, though, being right in there with the production.

As I'm sitting at the runway in the bar, the stripper comes up, starts flicking her boa at me (that is not a euphemism) and we're "interacting" when Piven as "Trevor" comes up and scares me off. For that interaction with the star I got an extra 25 bucks. If I had a line of dialogue it would have been a lot more money, but that may be why I heard a "huh?" tossed in there, as if I had said it. My guess is it was possibly dubbed in by someone who was already on the payroll and not an actor who would want more money.

I was barely visible on "Early Edition" and it went several seasons. I was visible but no bit player scene on "Turks," a mid season replacement that failed to get renewed. On "Cupid" it was my best "face time" yet, with the scene with the stripper and you guessed it, the show didn't last the season. There seemed to be a trend. The more "face time" I got, the faster the TV show went down. Actually I don't feel entirely responsible. I'm sure El Nino and a vast right wing conspiracy had something to do with it.

The one time I volunteered to be an extra and wasn't on the payroll was when the movie "Stir of Echoes" with Kevin Bacon came to Joliet to film. I thought it would be cool and my friend Bob Erck was already a hired extra on this job. The filming was at a hardware store and while the setting is Bacon in character buying some digging equipment, I never showed up on film, the victim of an editor's cut. However I am now one degree of Kevin Bacon, which is better than six. (That's kind of an obscure reference to the game "Six Degrees of Kevin Bacon" which itself is a takeoff on the Six Degrees of Separation claiming that everyone in the world is connected.)

It's mind-boggling when you realize that in one broadcast TV show, you can be seen by more people than the number who ever saw the most famous actor in the 1800s in their entire career!

Part of the fun of being an extra is talking with other extras, who will tell you of the other movies and television shows they've done. They're doing the work for different reasons. I found Monica, an attractive blond in her mid-20s who wanted to be a teacher but soured on that idea. She was out the night before a shoot and didn't get word of her early studio call until after one a.m. There was Angela, who wanted to be a professional actress. I suppose being an extra is a better route to that goal than just sitting in your house and hoping, but probably not much better. Extra work is not considered an avenue to acting. There's my friend Bob, the scientist/ metallurgist by day, and the extra by, well, also sometimes by day. He admired actors and was fascinated with the film and TV industry, but I think preferred more technical work. Both of us appreciated the fine culinary spread offered by the caterers.

Oh and there was also Adolph. He was a cook in a kitchen scene along with me in "Early Edition," but he insisted we call him "the Soup Nazi" that character from the show "Seinfeld." He wasn't the guy who played that part, but I suppose if someone named Adolph wants to be called "Soup Nazi," who am I to argue?

Speaking of food service, the extras ate apart from the crew. Part of that class system that seems so popular there. Ah, the glamour of show biz!

IF THIS IS THE BIG TIME, WHERE ARE THE CLOWNS AND ELEPHANTS? OH, THAT'S THE BIG TOP

IN SEPTEMBER OF 1997, I was still working at WKBM radio, south of Joliet, broadcasting mostly to the smaller communities in outlying areas southwest of Chicago. One day the manager came to me and wandered around the newsroom as he told me how there were things he loved about radio and things he didn't and that this was something he didn't love. (Okay, here it comes -- something I've heard too often) and they couldn't afford me anymore and so in a couple of weeks I would be out of a job. I'm sure the fact they were selling the station didn't play any part in that. I mean, how could the bottom financial line affect such generous people like this? Italics just don't convey sarcasm so I won't use them here.

People were telling me this could be best thing that ever happened to me and you probably know that's a hard sell when you are suddenly without an income, even if it's barely an income. Well, maybe, just maybe, though rarely, they could be right. Several opportunities actually came my way, including a big time radio gig, that television extra work I told you about and a chance to work with a radio legend.

Shortly after I left WKBM, I sent a resume to a Chicago station that was looking for a news production person. I got a call from WMAQ AM, a 50-thousand watt CBS owned all-news station and WMAQ tells me it looks like I have some writing ability and how about coming in and talking about it? Sure, sounds good to me, even if it is part-time. It was a 50-mile one-way drive and of course parking in downtown Chicago ain't cheap, but the job is offered to me to work as a newswriter on weekends. I entered the world of big city radio. This overnight success only took me 20 years, but in some ways I feel I fit right in. But then, after 20 years in radio I should fit right in.

Many there were quite qualified, while some were not, probably as with any business. There were some who seemed quite taken with their place in radio but for the most part it was a good environment. Of course, there were also those in their 20s who obviously got the break a lot earlier than I did. They seemed to know their job, though, and the system worked, though it was very fragmented. The news editor decided what stories were used in the hour and put the source material into the computer for it to be written. I would write something that might include sound cuts from the production person, and the anchor will read it and do some writing of their own. I might help the production person by processing a sound cut and the editor would do some writing. Once in a great while I did a live report on-air from the newsroom and regularly taped a report to air throughout the day. I was really glad to get on-air and my ability to do that is an added benefit for anchors or editors looking to put more "sound" in the newscasts.

WMAQ Radio studios were on the 6th floor of the NBC Tower. Jerry Springer taped his show in the same building. Maybe that explains the broken chairs in the lobby. (That's a joke)

As I've said, life is a series of moments and one of those "moments" came to me one Saturday in April 1998. I was asked at WMAQ to cover a speech being given by former presidential candidate and former Senator Bob Dole at Meigs Field, a small corporate plane airport on Chicago's lakefront. It's no longer there, (the airport, not the lake) if you're looking for a plaque with my name. I enjoy doing that but have yet to find one. But back to Dole, who was speaking on behalf of a senatorial candidate. After the speech I called in a live report from the site, then headed over to the south side of Chicago for the South Side Irish Parade. I did a live report from there, and briefly talked with secretary of State candidate Tim McCarthy. He was already known as the former Secret Service agent and then police chief who took the bullet for Ronald Reagan in March of 1981. He lost that Illinois race for secretary of State. After all of that reporting I headed back to the station.

I was in the "news cruiser" looking very official with 'WMAQ Radio News' written on the side, blue and white paint, and I'm traveling up Lake Shore Drive with the impressive Chicago skyline ahead of me. I think to myself, "I'm in the news cruiser of an all-news station in the third largest market in the country! I'm going to savor this."

Of course, that same "official car" can be embarrassing when you make a wrong turn, as I did, and had to back out of the wrong lane of an entrance ramp. Nobody particularly cared when I was in my nondescript Nissan.

Working for a 50,000 watt, clear channel station that covers several states was finally at least close to a network job. At least I had the chance that many don't get. Some get to big time radio in weeks, some, like me, take 20 years and, of course, some never get there. Eventually the station was dissolved in corporate maneuvering and after more than 70 years, "went dark" and disappeared from the face of Chicago.

That disappearance from the airwaves was after I left to move back to Arizona but nothing is forever anymore in any business. The closest you can come is probably a government civil service job or a tenured teacher position, which is also a government job. Even though I wasn't on the air very much at WMAQ I loved the small amount of recognition. That includes the time my new mail carrier said it was good to hear me back on the air. It's that kind of response that helps to make all of this worthwhile.

GOOD MORNING, AMERICAN.
OH, YOU MEAN ME

STAY IN ANY business long enough and you probably cross paths with some heavyweights. No, I never met George Foreman. I'm talking about broadcasting bigwigs.

I was still working at WMAQ in November 1998 when ABC went on strike. As a CBS employee that didn't mean a lot to me, but at ABC radio it meant the man who was copy editor for famed commentator Paul Harvey was on the picket line. My friend Gil Peters from WMAQ had been given the chance to fill in for the copy editor. There came a time around Thanksgiving that year when Gil was unable to do the job and they asked him whom he would recommend to take his place for a few days. He recommended a couple of people and the man who made the choice recognized my name and said I was fine for the replacement gig. It's all about contacts. Radio is really a relatively small circle of folks, though none of my relatives is in radio, as far as I know. Mr. Harvey's office overlooked Michigan Avenue, just across the river from the Tribune Tower and the Wrigley Building. I showed up for training with Gil and he filled me in on the duties. I had briefly met Mr. Harvey earlier at his studio and office while visiting Gil and was looking forward to working with him.

The first day on the job by myself Mr. Harvey was out of the office. Nationally syndicated broadcaster and Director of Chicago's Museum of Broadcast Communications Bruce DuMont, was in the studio doing a dry run, a sort of audition with the possibility of one day taking Mr. Harvey's place. I had actually met Bruce nine years earlier. Our paths crossed years before when I visited Chicago and the museum. On that day he probably noticed the KRKK/KQSW Wyoming call letters on my sweater. He graciously introduced himself and we spoke briefly. Now our paths crossed again at the Paul Harvey studio and office at 333 North Michigan and it was a pleasure to work with him. Again, radio is a small circle.

Paul Harvey's ABC Studio home on Michigan Avenue in Chicago overlooking the Chicago River

Each of my brief two days with Mr. Harvey in the office began before 4:30 a.m. One of the mornings I beat him in the door and I was in my office. I was standing over my desk looking down when suddenly from the hallway I hear, "good morning, American." I looked up and he was there smiling. I thought that was very cool. My own, "good morning, American."

My duties included going through the wire services and picking copy for him to use in his early newscast and noon news/commentary broadcasts. I gave him a stack of stuff and obviously he culled what he liked and put it together in his order and with his writing style; incidentally, a style produced in 1998 still on an IBM Selectric typewriter, using yellow paper with carbon paper. After he wrote his copy he would come into my office and hand it to me to proofread. I was somewhat daunted. I mean, Paul Harvey had just given me his copy for my approval. That's the "typo" editorial control (clever, huh?) I had, though nothing too extensive. I obviously didn't have veto power over anything he wrote or the order he wanted it, but I was to correct typos and he wanted to hear if a fact were wrong and I'm sure he would have been open to suggestions if something sounded unclear.

My desk in the outer office of the Paul Harvey studio and offices. That building out the window is the NBC tower where I was also working part time at WMAQ Radio.

Around the office Mr. Harvey liked to wear a smock, much like you would see on a pharmacist. But this one was blue and had an ABC emblem on the chest.

Before I worked those few days I had watched him deliver his news and commentary report and as a long time broadcaster myself I found it interesting to see he did voice warm up exercises before going on air and when the voice raised with his trademark "good day," so did his facial muscles.

Statue on display in the front of the Paul Harvey offices

I call myself a long time broadcaster but that's such a relative term. Mr. Harvey defined long term with a radio resume that dated back to high school and 1933. His association with ABC Radio Networks began in 1951. I consider it a "moment" in my career and one I can always look back on with a certain pride and with a warm feeling for the staff and Mr. Harvey and the way they welcomed me into the upper echelon of national broadcasting. For the most part, that's the way people in radio are. They're more than happy to talk with you and help you make the contacts you need. Sure, some are guided by pettiness and misguided ego, but down in the trenches you will find some great folks.

"EVEN MORE SEX THAN I CAN DESCRIBE." OKAY, NOW I CAN SAY IN THIS BOOK YOU'LL FIND "MORE SEX THAN I CAN DESCRIBE."

I NEVER KNEW sex scenes could be so easy to write. With quotes like this the book can be acceptable reading on nearly any campus, even in "safe zones."

EPILOGUE

IN HONOR OF QUINN MARTIN

HAVE YOU EVER watched old TV programs like "The FBI" or "Twelve O'Clock High?" The shows were divided into acts and at the end of a Quinn Martin production there would be an epilogue. I've talked radio so much, there's another one of my tributes to '60s television.

I'D BETTER CLOSE now as the postman is due. (That's how my Grandma Menke always signed off her letters.) I've warned you of the money situation in radio and you may hear, as an excuse (although a lame one), "well, that's the business." Ironically you may hear that from the next person up the line who's making three times what you are. You'll have experiences and "moments" and meet people you would never encounter in a career as a grocery clerk or some desk job. You may never be able to go out to dinner without cutting back on your other expenses, say fresh vegetables. I look back on decades in radio and media and my love/hate relationship. I think of the price I paid for it. Gas station owners across the country knew me by sight. Rental truck and trailer companies could call me by my first name and offer me volume discounts. I'm an expert at change of address cards and paid enough landline phone hook-up fees to be called Pa Bell. I know that's a really dated reference, but don't you feel good getting it? But if you didn't I'm afraid you'll have to look it up. Look for Ma Bell. That's what we liked to call her.

WOULD I RECOMMEND a career in radio? Frankly, it doesn't matter what I say. I wouldn't have listened when I was in my 20s and neither would some kid today. More importantly, if you need it badly enough no one can talk you out of it. If you can be talked out of it, you didn't really want it in the first place. To survive it, you have to want it in the first, second and 23rd place, and believe me, I've lived near 23rd place and you have to really want that too.

Radio can be highly rewarding work! Most importantly, if you're starting or changing any career, find something that if they didn't pay you, you would still do it for free. Whether it's radio or some other profession, follow the thinking of philosopher and teacher Joseph Campbell, who said, "follow your bliss." ***Go do it, and don't look back***.

###